Ecology is no longer a term known only to scientists.

Dr. Frank Fraser Darling here presents the truths we must face about the dependence of man on the natural world. Because his world is not one of political boundaries, his scope is truly international.

A pioneer ecologist of worldwide reputation, Sir Frank Fraser Darling has spent a lifetime studying the relationship of man to his environment all over the globe. He views the wilderness as a shrinking natural resource, no longer an environment to be conquered by man. He looks toward the future with a plan for conservation and a plea for man's responsibility to nature.

Sir Frank Fraser Darling was educated at the University of Edinburgh and is now Vice-President of the Conservation Foundation in Washington, D. C. He is author of many books in the environmental field, including WEST HIGHLAND SURVEY, PELICAN IN THE WILDERNESS, and with A. Starker Leopold, WILDLIFE IN ALASKA.

WILDERNESS
and
PLENTY

The Reith Lectures 1969

Sir Frank Fraser Darling

A BALLANTINE/FRIENDS OF THE
EARTH BOOK

BALLANTINE BOOKS, LTD.
An Intertext Publisher
LONDON ● NEW YORK

First U.S.. Printing: February, 1971
First U.K.. Printing: September, 1971

Cover photo by Ray Atkeson

Printed in Canada.

Ballantine Books, Ltd..
8 King Street
London, WC2E 8HS

Distributor: Pan Books, Ltd.

CONTENTS

WILDERNESS AND PLENTY

I

MAN AND NATURE

IF I WERE ASKED to interpret briefly what I mean by Wilderness and Plenty I would reply: population, pollution and the planet's generosity—meaning the history of man and the effect he has had, and is having, on the economy of nature since he appeared on the planet. These are closely interconnected themes, like the pattern of a fabric, throughout this book, and I propose to follow them through their intertwined complexity. Let us begin with ourselves.

The most significant event in the organic history of the Earth in the last 100,000 years has been the rise in the world population of human beings in the past two centuries. Man spent so long getting a foothold, and even when he had reached the gregariousness that civilization allowed, hazards were great. One might say that only then could the allegory of the Four Horsemen of the Apocalypse be conceived. We suddenly became aware that they rode, destroying the stability so newly gained. But the Earth seemed limitless; it is only 500 years or so since we discovered with certainty that the planet was globular and finite.

The shock of that discovery seems to have been more religious and philosophical than biological, until the inexorable biological consequences occurred in the colonization of the New World and the destruction of its indigenous but senile civilizations. The total world population of human beings was probably about 500 million at that time. It was less than 1000 million by A.D. 1800 when the Industrial Revolution had just begun. But what hits me most forcibly as a yardstick is that there are twice as many people on Earth now as there were when, as an inquiring youth, I first read *The Origin of Species*, Dean Inge's *Outspoken Essays* on eugenics and then Malthus on population. There are now about forty people to every square mile of the Earth's land surface, 3.6 thousand million in all according to latest United Nations estimates.

There will be nearly as many again by A.D. 2000.

When I was young, men still thought of going into the world's wilderness to carve out farms and ranches as a splendid thing to do, though my remembrance is that our aim was not an altruistic one of growing more food for the new millions, but that any food that you did grow would pay for the good life you had chosen for yourself.

This too has passed away with the memory of empires. Now, in straits almost of desperation, governments and United Nations agencies are feverishly carving up the remnants of nature's wilderness wherever it is thought possible to grow more food or hold more water for the increasingly articulate hungry millions. The cumulative impact of man on the face of the Earth has been considerable already: think of the dry, eroded Mediterranean region compared with that of Homer's heroes! Even he knew that his world was not so good as it was in the days before the Trojan War. The Sahara Desert is expanding all the time, not now by climatic change in that direction but through the grazing practices of man, which are themselves influenced by the impingements of settled agriculture. Yet we go on doing what history has clearly shown to be wrong, e.g. the current extension of cultivation into hilly districts and poorer soils in Africa, South America and Southeast Asia. The biological impact is mounting and the ecological consequences are giving concern to more and more people.

I suppose that I, like most other people, think I have lived through a particularly interesting period of history, an allowable conceit you will grant when we think how increasingly interesting history is becoming; but I have seen such changes of attitude among people generally considered intelligent and farseeing. Malthus was writing when there were less than 1000 million people on the globe, two sevenths of what there are now. He thought in terms of food production and one of his mistakes was that he did not conceive of the enormous advances that might be made in the methods of farming on both the physical and genetic fronts. Certainly the essays of Malthus instigated Darwin to gather his data on the theory of evolution by natural selection, but so far as human population was concerned, Malthus was politely laughed off, and sometimes not so politely. The population curve in England almost leveled out in the 1920s-30s and in Scotland it actually dipped. The empire took a lot of emigrants of course, but as so many of the wiseacres explained to us, one should know that the birthrate dropped as the standard of living rose. This is just a blind truism.

The desire for such horizon-widening artifacts as automobiles, radios and laborsaving gadgetry made people attempt a measure of family planning. In the better-educated classes the rise of feminism also helped to control the birthrate. Women wanted a career and civilized life as well as children. Men looked upon women as partners and people they liked living with rather than just treating them as housekeepers and brood mares. So, said the know-alls, we need not bother about undue growth of human population.

Dean Inge got himself called the Gloomy Dean for having the awkward perspicacity to see that not only was there a wide differential in the birthrate in civilized societies between the professional and the laboring classes, but that there was a great undeveloped world out there where any notion of family limitation was either nonexistent or repugnant.

Then came the Second World War, which turned topsy-turvy so many well-entrenched ideas, more than did the First War really. There was a rise in the birthrate in civilized countries, significant enough to produce the harassing post-war bulges in the educational systems. But in the so-called underdeveloped and nonindustrial countries there was not so much a rise in the birthrate as a fall in the deathrate with a steady birthrate.

Since the growth of medical knowledge in the nineteenth century there has always been a strong missionary zeal to cope with disease in far countries as well as to carry the Christian religion. Death rates were already gently falling by the time the Second War armies began to move into these places. Health measures then were of vital and immediate importance and some of these were not matters of personal attention but acts involving change in habitat. Malaria has always been a great killer, and once the vector was discovered by Sir Ronald Ross at the turn of the century it was inevitable that some substance would eventually be found which would be lethal to the mosquito and could be applied easily in malarial habitats. We all know the story of DDT and the way it enabled mankind to eliminate malaria in many countries. Ceylon is an excellent example and the results have been dramatic in doubling of population.

British Guiana in the Second War gave an even more dramatic exhibition through aerial spraying of DDT as a blanket operation. Infant mortality around 300 per thousand births was reduced to 67 and here, because malaria is also a debilitating disease, the birthrate rose. The standard of living in terms of calorie intake was about 1500 per day when the campaign began. No wonder there was a long period of political unrest, because before people get too weak to grumble at starvation they get angry. Wherever preventive medicine has had a chance to work in the tropics, there has been a rise in population beyond the increase in food production, and the immediate human situation has been an increase in squalor and stress. There has been far too little concomitant research on control of fertility. It is easy, of course, to talk from hindsight.

It is observable that when shortages of subsistence occur, people tend to congregate. They hear that food can be got in the cities or at the ports, and that is where they drift. The barrios of Lima in Peru and fevelas of Rio de Janeiro in Brazil are now notorious, abject aggregations of people without hope or social cohesion except that of similar plight. Calcutta is even worse, for that is where the food ships come and thousands are living their lives through lodged on the pavements. We are constantly troubled by the growth of large cities such as London and New York, where shortage of housing is chronic, but considered objectively there is still some sense of organic growth, for the incomers mostly come for work in a society that needs labor. But these tropical cities are growing at a much faster rate on no perceivable organic principle. There is that uncontrolled proliferation of cells as in cancer. As yet we have not found the cure.

Nor, indeed, do we know how to consider our reactions to this vast increase in world population. Do we withhold medical care and let folk die? Surely not, but even now, in our full consciousness of the need for birth control, we do not know how to apply the means. Contraception is a fairly sophisticated procedure, applied by the individual, and when it is attempted on a mass scale as in India, it barely scratches the surface of the problem.

The prospect seems inescapable that we face a future of continuing overpopulation and congestion. Civic effort seems incapable of dealing with the situation even as a holding operation. In London, the recent Notting Hill Report disclosed a revolting condition of overcrowding, shared rooms, shared houses, shared lavatories, shared squalor. The population of Britain is increasing and as a general phenomenon it does not seem to be greatly heeded; only in the particular instances where local government is faced with problems of overcrowding it is not fitted to cope with is the press of people felt. We accept immigrant populations to provide labor which the opinion of economics dictates that we need. Rehousing and urban renewal seem geared to a status quo and not to a curve of increase in numbers. More people live in conditions which, if they reflect, cannot be called home as they would wish it. Home, that lovely word understood by most races, even if you are a nomad in a yurt, but particularly by those folk who have a sense of place. *Oikos*, the Greeks called it, and we have made the root the basis of our words *ecology* and *economics*.

There are fashions in words, and ecology is one of these, much newer than economics, but it is being bandied about until people are growing sick of it before they know what it means— the science of the organism in relation to its whole environment, in relation to other organisms of different species, and to those of its own kind. These two fields, ecology and economics, presently so far apart in outlook, must sometime come nearer together, and may that be soon. The economic factor looms so large that people in power use it as if it were some real power, one of a trinity with God and Satan. Folk and family are forgotten in some figment called gross national product, expressed in dollars and pounds sterling. God and Satan have been losing out in the battle of ideas but the economic factor has gained such power as almost to dictate a truncated existence for the many. This is called the greatest good for the greatest number.

Of course, horizons have widened for almost everyone except the old, but, where there is overcrowding, the fuller life which education and growing knowledge make possible is truncated to an existence in which stress ceases to be the stimulus, which is the natural and proper function of stress, to become an organic depressant of beauty, of the romantic spirit which is the pearl of our human heritage.

Man is probably the most adaptable animal on Earth, but he is still an animal to whom natural laws apply until his ingenuity manages to overcome them in part. Comparative anatomy and physiology are still valid studies and the ecologist extends them to behavior and environment. What lemmings are supposed to do when they get too many has become almost apocryphal and the simile has been used often enough to prophesy the course of human behavior by people who have no understanding of lemmings or their environment or the organism-environment relation. Lemmings are small rodents living in a fairly simple Arctic and sub-Arctic environment. As Charles Elton pointed out over forty years ago, fluctuation of populations of Arctic animals is more pronounced than in the temperate and tropical zones. Rodents display this cyclicism particularly and give us good subjects for investigation. An American ecologist, Paul Errington, trapped muskrats in Minnesota to pay for his university education and then, with characteristic brilliance, made the muskrat the central animal of his studies. He knew the creatures so intimately that, in the spirit of science, he could learn much more. He noted their capacity to live together and increase. The philo-progenitive nineteenth century would have been charmed. Then the idyll begins to fade, for the animals become more quarrelsome and show signs of stress. The inquiring ecologist finds gastroenteritic conditions prevalent in the population, and going still further, discovers hormonal imbalance. Here is evidence of excessive stress. Numbers decrease and the picture is of thin distribution. Then the cycle starts again.

Whether they are muskrats, lemmings or field voles, we see the animals following the pattern of Elton's and Errington's observations. The common factor is stress.

Man is not a muskrat but he bears some comparison. Both species are gregarious but crowding brings about psychosomatic and social behavioral disorders. The quality of adaptability in man is immense, so that density of population as such is no absolute criterion. There is a big difference, indeed, between high density and overcrowding. Good manners allow great density without stress; good sanitation and hygiene allow considerable density without a high incidence of gastroenteritis. Good town planning allows smooth flow of people. But what is all this if everyone has not a hole of his own?

The physical environment, that which we see, hear, feel, taste and smell, is a field in which the influences on human beings are more debatable because people are so different—their individual likes and dislikes, their culture and social backgrounds. Industrial societies would seem to need high density for economic convenience, and we know that industrialization seems to be the most significant reducing factor in the birthrate. Here is paradox again. Most nations seek industrialization for economic reasons. But the environmental conditions sought for by industrial development are rarely achieved by the many. Despite the attendant fall in birthrate, population still increases beyond absorptive capacity because the death rate falls and life expectancy increases. Our traditionally allotted span of three-score years and ten seems now too generous in an industrial welfare state. We should relieve so much stress on the productive age groups if we were out of the way at sixty.

But few if any of us really wish to look upon ours or any other society as an efficient conglomerate of production-consumption units. We seek the good life, and many of us at some time or other have had the illusion that there was once a golden age of man. The good life for a larger proportion of the population of any country is not an illusion but an ideal capable of being achieved. Indeed, we should never lose sight of it or be in any way content with the half-lives so many are compelled to lead.

We can admit that the environment we have inherited and which we are still fashioning can be so far improved that a higher density of population than that of the present will find the world a more satisfying place in which to live. But there can be no valid doubt that population increase and environmental pollution are the world's biggest problems today. We have, rightly as I think, ceased to be complacent to accept disease as a natural check; we abhor infanticide of normal newborn babies, which must have been a considerable population check when female children were preferentially exposed.

Sterilization of men and women by choice is a growing practice in many developed and developing countries; active birth control is increasing; but there are dangers here, in that the less responsible sections of populations will beget an undue proportion of coming generations. There are fiscal possibilities, though taxes can be gathered only from those who have the wealth to pay them. Indeed, in some developed countries we still have cash benefits *for* having large families. Education must have much to do, and that early life, in persuading people to decide for themselves on the necessity for limitation of numbers of children; civics and a reproductive ethic should be inculcated together, helped by government action based on the acceptance of such limitation rather than on vote-catching. The ethical decision must come from within.

In few governments in the world are there any clear policies or directives. They recognize the cogency elsewhere but are frightened and expedient at home. What becomes particularly hurtsome is when palings in a black African country are daubed with legends to the effect that birth control propaganda is a white attempt at genocide of the black.

I see no early relief to the world's population explosion but I feel active thinking and working on preservation of the few untouched plant and animal communities and their habitats, the positive sense in which I am using the word *wilderness*, and on the rehabilitation of the existing degraded environments in which so many live is possible and immediately desirable. Derelict landscape is *not* wilderness. This **is** indeed a world problem, to be faced by the world as a whole—the United Nations preferably. The economic factor is enormously powerful, setting firm against firm in cutting down production costs and caring little about disposal of wastes. Country is set against country in getting the world markets; the materialists' creed is that industry must not be handicapped by idealistic policies of pollution control. One African country has recently pointed out that the measures of control of pollution suggested to it as being desirable when beginning to industrialize would come better if the European countries were doing the same. We are doing something, but not nearly enough, even to save our face.

I would say, in all modesty, that ecology has its particular contribution to make in understanding the environment man has made for himself in the heavily populated areas of the Earth, and from that point methods could be devised toward conservation of that which is good and rehabilitation of that which is bad. I would think this nearer to being human ecology than aspects of those sciences which already carry their own good names. Sociology, I think, would deal with those phenomena of social implosion, an expression which perhaps better describes the social consequences of what is commonly called the population explosion.

Even if populations in the developed countries were to remain steady and gently to fall, there would still occur the tendency toward urbanization. Living successfully and gracefully in towns is an art, civilization by definition, and the incomer from rural life has much to learn. This I found for myself when I went to live in New York after my island years and the later expansive comforts of an English country house.

I truly believe there is a considerable need for medicine, ecology, architecture, landscape and town planning and conservation to combine in some fields of our changing world. Stress and psychosomatic diseases stem in part from environmental factors the ecologist senses but cannot state in medical terms. The landscape and town planner should be combining ecology with his sense of order. I sometimes think architecture should be the first subject taught to a child, giving him bricks of good and progressive design, even if he does build them in impossible ways and push them down. He might then be more positively intolerant when he grows up. Good architecture conveys a sense of well-being and Hogarth's delight in the serpentine line was well based. The sharply angular townscape we know so well and the plethora of sheer bad design offend the sensitive excruciatingly, but somewhere medicine and psychology could tell us that even the insensitive are being affected, made less successful human beings.

Conservation has traditionally been concerned with natural resources, particularly the animate ones, and with habitats of animal and plant communities, but this science of applied ecology must now logically include the human species as an organism to be conserved. This is no paradox, for we hold to the principle that children born healthy should live, and that as adults they should be able to express their potential for themselves and for all. Conservation is a synthesizing applied social science crossing the boundaries of all branches of culture, not least the arts, in its observational study of communities.

From earliest times men have lived in communities—families, clans, villages, towns, cities. Today in Britain and the United States nearly three quarters of the people have left the land to live in urban fashion, in which technological change has far outstripped man's slow biological evolution. How this has come about, and the effect it has had on the natural wilderness, is the main topic of the next chapter.

II

THE IMPACT OF MAN
ON HIS ENVIRONMENT

IN THE FIRST CHAPTER I implied that although man is not yet lord of creation, he is undoubtedly the dominant species on our planet. Moreover he is such a complex creature that he is constantly challenging and altering his environment. As soon as he became man, and we need not bother just when it was, he began to alter the face of the natural world as it was until then. While he remained a hunter-foodgatherer he was little more than another indigenous animal. But as soon as he burned wood to keep warm he was consuming it in a different way from natural decay, with different consequences.

When he used fire as an aid to driving wild animals into places where he could kill them more easily, and burned bush to encourage hoofed animals to graze on the young grass which followed, he had begun his ceaseless attrition of the natural wilderness.

At first men were presumably few and they evolved on an Earth that had already been amassing biological wealth for millions of years. Their burning of habitat for hunting was, of course, a prodigious expenditure of organic matter for momentary expedience.

And as the human species increased, more men meant more burning. The same ground was burned too often and this led to impoverishment of the broad spectrum of species of plants. Biological productivity and ecological wealth rest on the wide variety of species, which means flexibility and unconscious cooperation within the whole ecosystem. When man alters natural ecosystems by design or ignorance they are usually simplified or made less complete and lose something of their holistic quality of resistance to invasion by foreign species.

The Neolithic Revolution was indeed that for some areas, as natural habitats became fields for the production of a single crop. There was an initial loss through this cultivation until man learned to sustain his arable land, but again, the Earth was big and men still relatively few.

Domestication of animals must have caused some measure of overgrazing very soon, for the great advantage of domestication was having the animals where you wanted them when you wanted them, and usually in greater density than they would be found in nature. Throughout history overgrazing has been a great creator of deserts, and still is. Nomadic animal husbandry was a considerable technical advance, following the grass, using different animals for different habitats. Maintenance of these grazing lands of several kinds was necessary for survival of tribe and culture.

The advent of the Bronze Age gives us rather more to bother about in the way of impact on habitat. Native copper was originally found in lumps on rocks in Anatolia. It could be hammered by stones into useful and decorative artifacts. Then it was discovered that metal could be extracted from ore by heat and some genius of the region discovered the advantages of alloying the rather soft copper with tin. This needed more heat still, and more heat needed more fuel, and that meant less forest. Man was truly in business as a consumer of the planet's riches of natural resources. The discovery of iron and ability to work it enlarged the whole scope of the smelting industry, at the same time increasing the strain on the fuel-producing forests.

Making pots was probably a woman's discovery, but it is man who streamlines processes and fosters efficiency of production. The roots of the notion of mass production go down to our technological beginnings. The Chinese above all others perfected clays for different kinds of pots and learned the art of reaching intense heats in kilns, and of regulating heat. Once more the forests provided the fuel and China today has a continuous problem of barren hills and silting rivers, stemming from the centuries when, it is recorded, the sky of Chekiang was black with the smoke of the busy kilns.

The introduction of coal—fossilized energy from the past—must have given breathing space to the world's forests near to populated areas but it was almost too late. England's forests were in tatters by A.D. 1700 and those of Scotland were next assailed. Ships carried cargoes of iron ore up the long sea lochs of the West Highlands to be smelted in furnaces fed by oak and pine. And the process continued elsewhere.

A fundamental point we can observe in impact of man on natural habitats is that it is most severe and destructive when some natural product of the habitat, such as timber, or some technical product, like China's pots, is exported from the region. The cedar forests of the Lebanon have gone; Solomon and the ancient Egyptians long before him had imported the timber in quantity. The onslaught of the nineteenth century on the forests of North America was so shocking that I have the feeling that that was the reason for the early rise of their sense of conservation.

These problems are of course not confined to temperate lands. Tropical forests have always been treated extractively and with little heed for consequences. The trees are so monumental and the forests gives such a sense of permanence that the fragility of this oldest life form on Earth is not generally realized. But tropical rain forest is primarily a natural photosynthetic factory and store of cellulose; protein production as animal life is secondary and incidental. For many thousands of years the floor of the forest has been sheltered from the sun and within it there is an intricate and efficient conversion of organic matter into nutrients for new growth. When, after felling, the floor is laid bare to the tropical sun there is rapid oxidation of the soil which, indeed, proves to be scanty and poor once the organic matter and the organisms achieving the cycles of decay and renewal are gone. Yet a most wasteful felling and pushing aside of forest in the Matto Grosso of Brazil is going on at present.

The pressure of numbers of people has had another immense impact in the drainage of wetlands around the globe. This is another setting-back of the natural wilderness. The process has gone on throughout history to create both more cultivable land and navigable waterways. Wetlands constitute one of the world's most biologically productive life forms, and, in this instance, of protein in the shape of animals. Much of this animal life provides desired human food but, of course, it needs catching by fishermen and hunters. Where the soil is alkaline peat, as it is in the Fens of eastern England, it becomes rich agricultural ground after drainage. But it also shrinks, so diking and pumping are necessary to keep the water away. Recently in the United States there has been a tendency to revert from the policy of draining wetlands to one of allowing them to refill and become protein producers again. This policy is perhaps possible today only in an affluent country that produces grain surpluses, and where wetlands and their wildlife have a recreational value.

The Dutch are also changing the face of their country by playing with water, that ingrained masculine amusement. But it is of a different order, surely constructive and inspiring. Large areas of land are being won from shallow salt water of no great biological productivity, and research has shown how the land can be made into good agricultural soil. What is even more inspiring, the art of landscape architecture, linked with the thoughtful establishment of nature reserves, is making these new lands into pleasant living places. There has been imagination at work as well as skill, which conjunction, I feel, has not been the usual way that man has been changing the face of the planet through the years.

So much then for some of the broad changes that man has wrought in his environment. Let us now pause for a moment to consider what sort of a species man is, or would like to be.

In nature, he is omnivorous, the male catching the protein by hunting and the female fathering the fruits of the Earth. Later, the horse cultures of the steppes and those rich lands of the Crimea and Ukraine lived largely from the produce of their herds and flocks, and there are cultures in the Upper Nile that still do. Such people live where man belongs, at the top of a short food chain of grass-animals-man. Agricultural man changed this natural order to a situation where he himself feeds to some extent direct on the seeds of cereal grasses: wheat, rye, oats and barley. As time progresses and numbers of men increase, protein gets harder to come by, and the human species has become more and more a direct consumer of carbohydrate (starch), a more abundant derivative from the changed ecosystem, but in nutritional terms a devalued one. The more numerous people become the more likely are they to be depressed to the state of being starch eaters. So population increase forces the conversion of protein-producing ecosystems into starch-producing agriculture, and that magic touch of a higher standard of living which will reduce the birthrate continues to hang just in front of the donkey's nose.

We have had lessons from the past. Salaman of Cambridge pointed out many years ago what happens in countries which, as it were, sold their soul to the potato—ancient Chile, eighteenth- and nineteenth-century Ireland and the West Highlands and Islands of Scotland. The standard of living was desperately reduced and numbers rose inordinately. But the lessons are not heeded. Let me give you another example of projected change, this time in Africa. The Kafue and Chambeshi Flats in Zambia not only sustain herds of a close-herding antelope but their lagoons carry an extraordinary wealth of freshwater fish. Indeed the development of the fisheries has been one of the African success stories in protein production, but the antelope are losing out badly through lack of a proper policy of conservation which would harvest them carefully as a valuable protein crop. Then, of course, we have had the intention to turn the flats into wheat fields, and finally, they may go under water in a dam. A contemporary example of this way of thinking would be the Bahr el Ghazal region of the Upper Nile; the country of the rivers, which its name means, is potentially one of the richest protein-producing areas of the world, but the starch growers have already got 8000 acres as an experimental plot for rice. The Dinka are a fine race of tall Nilotics, living in symbiosis with their beautiful cattle and the wild game. Will a larger number of rice-fed Dinka living in a deteriorating habitat be a more contented people? I doubt it. Starch and sedition go together.

Another impact on the face of the Earth by men's activities is interference with drainage. This has happened as spoil-moving equipment has grown more powerful. The coal measures of Britain are not only defaced by mine refuse dumps and storage piles but considerable acreages around them are often waterlogged. The National Coal Board appears to be doing an impeccable job of clearing up and re-creating good landscape following their open-cast mining, which makes it more difficult to understand the dichotomy of mind shown by the board in declining to accept a continuing intention to clear away the mine refuse dumps and their attendant bogs—these oppressive and depressing monuments of the age of laissez faire.

Britain has been spared strip mining and auger mining for coal, but the hills of Kentucky are being scarred by this utterly ruthless and extractive process. Downstream the good arable lands along the Ohio River are being spoiled by the silt blocking the waterway. Here, too, is another dichotomy, for the large consumer of this coal is that environmentally-conscious body, the Tennessee Valley Authority. Should a state boundary act as a blindfold to what is happening on the other side of the watershed? Our world is too constricted now for any country or authority to ignore concern for the resources of a neighbor and say, "I am not my brother's keeper."

I want now to refer to two effects of industrialization that have had profound ecological effects. While human populations were small the use of rivers as natural sewers was perhaps of little consequence. With the coming of industry the situaton changed rapidly. Industry was quick to misuse the force of gravity plus flow of water to dump its wastes into the rivers, with immediate unpleasant results. In my younger days the whole valley of the Esk in Midlothian used to stink with the effluent of paper mills, and if the rivers of the state of Maine are flown over today in a light airplane the pollution and obstruction of the rivers from pulp mills are obvious. At the same time, England is trying to reduce the backlog of neglect; the Thames is a cleaner river than half a century ago despite a greatly increased population living on its banks. It is conceivable that the salmon will run up the Thames again someday. But I shall have more to say later about pollution of environment.

The other, and most regrettable, impact of man on the natural environment, quite distinct from the pollution aspect, although there are examples of direct linkage, is the creation of dereliction. This is truly ecological disaster. Dereliction is an ecosystem set back to beyond its pioneer stage with little hope of return, and to such a picture is usually added the hardware of humanly created detritus. Through man's history war has been an arch creator of dereliction; some of that wrought by Genghis Khan has not been set right yet in such places as Transoxiana, Afghanistan and Persia. The ancients created much beauty and ecological repose as conscious acts, such as the Persian gardens which give us the word *paradise,* and the oases and irrigated lands of the Central Asian snow rivers. Balkh, Merv, Bokhara and Samarkand were university towns of beauty till the Mongols came. They have not yet recovered. Nevertheless, the general emotional aftermath of the dereliction of war is to rebuild with a considerable idealism which quickens effacement of ruin. We have seen this in our own time and sometimes these re-creations have been heroic, like the old square in Warsaw.

The derelictions of the Industrial Revolution, produced around the world in only 200 years, have received little consideration or idealism. I can never quite understand why, when they have occurred, industry, government and folk should endure them with such callousness, fatalism and insensitivity. People still speak of wildness in a derogatory way, almost as if it were outmoded in human estimation—wilderness which carries the nobility of nature—yet until our day few people have voiced their detestation effectually of the desolation of the land and of the spirit caused by the arrogance of industrial dereliction.

John Barr, in a recently published book called *Derelict Britain,* tells us that we are still adding ten acres a day to the dereliction. What sort of people are we that, in a period of rising numbers, of affluence and mobility, and much-desired recreational space, we can filch land from posterity and turn it into squalor at the rate of ten acres a day? Government and local authorities have the legislation enabling them to tackle dereliction, but in fact most are logrolling, acting fragmentarily with a maximum of show, rather like funeral horses trained to trot magnificently at a pace slower than a walk. Not everywhere, of course, and I shall return to examples of rehabilitation. Sometimes, also, hawthorn bushes take over dereliction willy-nilly and birdsong is heard again, but, in general, derelict landscapes remain to foster psychosomatic disease by their primary violation of the eye. Bricks are so urgently needed for homes and work places that no one could be antibrick, but this profitable industry, along with its brother cement, is a spectacular creator of dereliction. Could we not have some environmental socialism, whereby the dereliction-producing industries would forgo a portion of their profits to devote to the rebuilding of landscape? In the ultimate good achieved I believe the social and political cost would be small. I think, indeed, that we need to develop some yardstick for human content; to be able to measure the lesser degree of discontent and psychosomatic disease in rehabilitated environments. This is the ulti-mate concern of politics.

With bricks and cement goes gravel, and such are the demands of construction in the Thames Valley and elsewhere that gravel diggings have created lakes. Fortunately some of these have escaped dereliction from an early moment be-cause numerous wading and swimming birds, great opportunists that they are, have taken over the diggings and drawn to them that now con-siderable body of opinion, the bird watchers. Sometimes the lakes have been large enough for sailing as a recreation, and with some imagina-tive planting for amenity, the sites have become assets to the community. The situation is less happy when the local council buys the water-filled emptiness for the deposition of refuse, ultimately creating sterile land fit only to take more buildings. It is all a question of difference between an ecological approach, a very simple one linked with a romantic outlook, and an unimaginative, unbiological one concerned only with keeping down the rates. The gravel firms themselves are under planning control and are committed to leave acceptable landscapes. In-sofar as they do this, they are to be commended.

I was recently in Alaska, attending the public hearings on the projected building of an 800-mile pipeline from the Arctic Ocean to Valdez on the Pacific Ocean. Nearly twenty years ago I traveled Arctic Alaska pretty thoroughly when the Office of Naval Research was exploring for oil west of this new great strike at Prudhoe Bay. The passage of caterpillar trains across the tundra, the dumps of oil drums, the filth of camps on permafrost were not very pretty, and on one occasion my colleague and I dug a trench in the frozen tundra, gathered up a year's expenditure of food cans strewn around the tent site and buried them. A useless gesture, doubtless, but I am still glad we did it.

Now, the activity is terrific. Hundreds and thousands of acres of Arctic tundra will no longer rear phalaropes, sandpipers, lemmings and snowy owls, but are being reinforced to take drilling rigs, make permanent campsites and so on. Many more cat trains are going on what will be a permanent road one day, and there are about a thousand flights a day to the north slope of the sublime Brooks Range.

Here is going to be impact in a big way. Whether we like it or not, we live in our era and that oil is going to come out. The world does not need that oil right now, but the world political factor which is also so potent an ecological factor makes it expedient that the rigs get going, the pipe line be built, and the 1000-foot tankers get moving through the Northwest

Passage, even though Canada is bothered about possible accidents in those narrow seas. Oil of the Middle East is subject to the political vagaries of impulsive, compulsive peoples who can upset the world situation at any moment they choose. Diplomacy and duplicity are not far apart where oil is in debate. The Alaskan strike gives the chance of more stability, so it must be developed. It could indeed be a factor in world peace. But what is going to happen to a large and biologically important area of Arctic wilderness?

It is no good looking back over our shoulder. We simply cannot stop oil development but we can do our utmost to canalize it and prune wasteful movement and development over the fragile habitat of the tundra. Till recently the state of Alaska was poor, now it is potentially rich and is desperately eager to get its fingers onto the contracts and subcontracts, the land speculation and all the rest. The state wants to get the land for itself from the federal government for the whole 800-mile length of the pipeline. There are lots of eager quick-buck men in Alaska. But there is also a surprisingly large number of people dedicated to the conservation of the Alaskan environment. There are 586,000 square miles and only a quarter of a million people, over 20 percent of them natives. The

far-seeing minority, extremely well informed
and enjoying a high scientific prestige, have
forced the federal government to hold these
public hearings.

It is certain that the pipeline will come, but
the group, calling for postponement and much
better survey and research than has been applied so far, point out that the route passes
through a series of changes in permafrost conditions and that it crosses an active earthquake
region. Each mile of pipeline will contain half
a million gallons of hot oil. What is the risk of
fractures? Breakdown could make the *Torrey
Canyon* a drop in the ocean by comparison. The
oil in the pipeline will be hot. How far will it
affect the immediate ground climate of the pipeline? How good will the insulation be? Melting
of permafrost could cause a good deal of erosion
and landsliding, as well as fracture. To prevent
the mistakes of the past, serious questions have
to be asked now and answers found. The federal
government will do an honest posterity-minded
job in this because it realizes that oil development on the scale it is nowadays is no local
affair.

The United States has had the salutary lesson
of the Santa Barbara oil disaster to make her be
more careful in Alaska. The geological forma-
tions in the Santa Barbara channel are unstable

and the Department of Interior was advised against allowing drilling in those waters. But the prize was so great that the advisers were over-ruled. Now the problem is to seal the disturbed strata against further seepage. The costs of this mistake in policy and failure in technology are going to be immense. One good thing to have come from this disaster is the extra caution the present administration is taking, and the penalties of costs are being set where they belong. But how soon will the underwater wonderland return? This was an area worthy of marine national park status.

Oil in our world is an international commodity and concern. So is man's environment an international commodity and concern. The disfiguring rash of nationalism which has assailed the world has set up political factors which exemplify my thesis that politics must never be neglected as a profound ecological factor. Politics could be benign, of course, and should be, but usually they are not. UNESCO held its Biosphere Conference in Paris in 1968 and we were impressed by the interest taken by the developing countries in Africa and Asia. In 1972 the United Nations will hold a conference at ministerial level, designed for action. For myself, I have no doubts of the intention and earnestness of nations to act well and dress well, as it were. But time, it seems to me, is not on our side. Even by the 1972 conference there will be over 150 million more mouths in the world, all of whom will be demanding of technology, "Give us more . . ."; not just food, but more of everything. So technology is forced to beget more technology and this exponential growth and what it implies is the main topic of the next chapter.

III

THE TECHNOLOGICAL
EXPONENTIAL

I WAS TALKING in the previous chapter of the impacts of man on his environment, coming historically—and prehistorically as well—into the present day. The ecological consequences of technology since the Industrial Revolution are still the burden of what I want to say now, but it is difficult to avoid some reflection on what technology is doing to the nature of man himself. Man, as distinct from woman the family craftworker, likes steady work rather less and brings his inventive mind to easing craft processes. I am sure man invented the potter's wheel and the lathe, and then carried on patterns which woman had conceived in the first place. As I have said before, the male of the human species has an innate tendency to streamline and mass produce.

Leonardo's drawings show us how far man had got by the time of the Renaissance in the way of transmitting power by cogwheels and directing it at right angles by beveling the cogs. There was no dearth of ingenious engines but the power was wanting. The eighteenth century was all ready for an access of power beyond that of wind and falling water when James Watt made steam drive an economical engine which was capable of doing more than pump water out of mines in Cornwall.

The Industrial Revolution was on immediately, the biggest factor of change the world has known. Steam applied to locomotion created a half-mobile world and might have detracted from the craft of the sea had not the engineers of the Clyde braved those incredible difficulties of making steam piston engines drive ships. But coal was cumbrous stuff and greater efficiency was constantly sought. Hydrocarbon oil could be won more easily than coal and Benz made the technical step forward of devising an internal combustion engine which made use of the almost academic researches of Faraday and his kind in electricity. Technology and invention run ahead, creating an inexorable momentum. But a momentum in a known, appreciated, desired direction; or a juggernaut spinning this way and that unpredictably? Of one thing we can be almost sure: each inventor in every field would be convinced that his idea put into practice would be for human good.

Our Greek derivation in western civilization gave us the reason which has guided our science, but the Judaic-Christian background has given us a man-centered world. Our technology is a monument to the belief that Jehovah created us in his image, a belief which of course had to be put that way to express the truth that man created Jehovah in *his* own image. The resources of the planet were for man, without a doubt. They could have no higher end than to serve man at the behest of Jehovah. There could be no doubt of the rightness of technology. At least, that is the way we have interpreted Christianity, though in its earlier years there was more feeling of man for the natural world.

Science, as our perception of the natural laws of the universe which we are still discovering, is the basis on which technology advances. Science isn't easy, because it involves a highly intellectual approach and a capacity to lay aside earlier belief and to think anew. Science is neutral and distinctly impersonal when it is soundly conceived. Technology is not science but the application of scientific principles to physical problems, very much man-centered. There is nothing impersonal about technology. Moreover, technology is fascinating: it works. What a blessing it is!

I am not being sardonic, because I live in my era. But I am one of the least technical of men except that I do like to know what scientific principles are behind the new gadgetry of living, even if I do not use it all—quite. Yes, technology is a lot easier than science to understand, and it commands immense respect from the species that has created it. Its capacity for efficiency and still more efficiency as new materials are discovered or synthesized and new scientific discoveries applied increases all the time. Once an advanced technology gets going it creates new demands in machines, things and materials, and so grows geometrically.

Then the whole modern background of technology begins to impinge seriously not only on the natural environment, whose only conscious guardian is man, but on the expanded and immense population of the species that created technology. A harassed minister of government may be perfectly convinced that some new industrial development will spoil something in the natural environment but—he will grimace apologetically and plead that we cannot afford to stand in the way of progress. That nineteenth-century conception of inevitable and absolute progress is still believed and it pushes us forward rather than leads on to that which we truly desire. Technology is apt to condition us psychologically so that man becomes its servant, no longer its creator and master. The automobile gets faster, trucks get larger, roads belatedly get wider, but country lanes are no longer for a pedestrian and the advance of mechanical agriculture has meant the loss of footpaths and removal of hedgerow trees. Efficiency demands it. The supersonic airliner *must* be produced simply because it can be. If you cannot sleep through it all, wear earplugs or something but do not grumble in the path of progress.

Jehovah has been steadily losing out since the Renaissance though he has fought a good rearguard action. In our century we have seen the mantle of Jehovah passed to Science with a capital S. But Science, as I say, is impersonal and is but truth and understanding as we see it at any one time. The pursuit of science still has humanistic qualities, and many scientists, though not subscribing to any notion of a Jehovah, nevertheless bow to the unknown and unknowable, the Divine Ground that the mystics of all religions and races acknowledge. Technology, on the other hand, is not impersonal; it is not of nature but of man, and, now that it is showing power to direct man as a species, is becoming Technology with a capital *T*—the new god, man's creation of an extension of himself to which he seems inclined to relinquish his power of free will which we have prized so much and accepted as being part of our difference, our apartness, from the animal world. It is not thought impossible anymore that a computer could be constructed which by thinking in its own amoral, rapid, electronic fashion could outwit us.

Leaving philosophy aside for a moment, let me take an example of an industry that illustrates what I have in mind—oil. And what I have to say is said in the realization that I contribute to whatever the oil industry is doing in shaping our world. Mine is a two-car family and I shall probably continue to go well over forty miles an hour when driving. This means I am using leaded gas. I also fly an average of 50,000 miles a year in airliners, so I am well and truly committed to oil. Oil is now the great motive fuel and, supplemented by natural gas, is becoming preponderantly our main heating fuel. The oil industry is truly international, either by the fortuitous geography of the oilfields or because the markets for the oil are often where there are no oilfields. The United States has a wealth of oilfields in the states bordering the Gulf of Mexico. There are many fields offshore from California. The Middle East is extremely rich; Russia has the Caspian and Volga fields and her own Arctic Ocean finds. The oil fields of Southeast Asia were one of the hopes of Japan in the 1940s. Now there is the new and vast Arctic Ocean strike in Alaska.

The oil industry is a good example of what I have called the technological exponential. To build cars you need steel and aluminum, plastics and rubber. Rubber-growing used up a lot of tropical wilderness, and now petroleum itself is needed as a raw material in the manufacture of synthetic rubber. The oil industry takes over from the older chemical industry and gives us many other things, detergents and plastics.

The great car assembly lines create aggregations of people, new towns, new roads, services, recreational facilities and so on. Technological growth, as I say, is exponential. People call this the expanding economy and feel pretty smug about it. The gross national product looks better every year, but what of the other side of the coin?

We are taught that matter is indestructible, and the axiom applies to the products of technology. Junk heaps may offend the eye, and because sight is the foremost of human senses, these may well be dealt with early in the approaching chaos. Worn-out automobiles in huge piles impress us with our capacity for producing waste, time waste, something which we are not prepared to recycle. Plastics seem indestructible. But there are substances left which are less obtrusive visually, the corrosive products of combustion and the soluble pollutants of water. Out of sight, out of mind can, however, be dangerous because pollution has insidious effects on human health, and on the persistence of ecosystems that have an unseen function in maintaining life and purifying environments.

Population and pollution are the two great problems of our age, and pollution is a function of population increase, though it need not necessarily be so. Most pollution comes from getting rid of wastes at the least possible cost. We are still using our rivers as sewers as were our forefathers tens of thousands of years ago, but there are more of us doing so many more complicated things. Some parts of the chemical industries that emitted noxious and corrosive fumes had to do something about it quite soon, but not before they had devastated many square miles of pleasant country. They installed "scrubbers" on their effluent routes and some found there was value even in whatever it was they scrubbed out. But whenever wastes could be blown off or run off, the economic factor—a term ill used in this sense—has been the criterion on whether pollutants of air and water were removed at source or released. We were not prepared to pay the price of our technology, the cost of cleaning up after ourselves. Those 250,000 acres of dereliction in Britain are just the bare bones of our degradation; the most subtle effects of air and water pollution have not been presented in any national balance sheet but they are dreadful in the real meaning of that word. Their acreage is far greater.

There are examples of some correction through the advance of technology, for do remember that if the will of the people is ultimately that the environment of man shall be clean and decent, it will be technology that will be our handmaiden in achieving it. In my young days the Pennine Chain was a region of small farms on sour soil trying to produce milk for the manufacturing districts. Here was initially calcium-deficient ground on the millstone grit, a bad start, but the farmers could get lime fairly cheaply from the kilns on the adjacent carboniferous limestone. But Manchester and its satellites and Sheffield and all the rest were belching out a huge tonnage of sulfur dioxide into the air, which, combining with the heavy rainfall, ultimately deposited on the land a quantity of sulfuric acid far greater than could be neutralized by agricultural dressings of lime.

Today there are good roads and milk tankers to move the milk quickly from areas much better fitted for milk production to the centers of population. The distance between cow and consumer can be hundreds of miles now, and those Pennine farmers are less harassed men than they were. But no one will dispute that there is still too much sulfuric acid falling in the industrial north.

There are some forms of almost unrestricted pollution that are growing rather than declining and some of them are more dangerous than sulfuric acid. As the chemical industry expanded in the years after the Second World War many new products that pleased most of us were introduced. Synthetic detergents were an example of the welcome we gave to a cleanser more effective than soap, especially in hard water. Then those of us who lived in the country found the bacteria in our septic tanks were not doing their work anymore. They did not like detergents. Public sewage works fared no better. Many of us remember the foam that covered the rivers in the fifties. The chemists had not thought far enough ahead. Detergent pollution of water became so bad that industry had to deal with the problem as an urgent ad hoc research. In a short time chemists reached a solution by developing a different molecular structure which could be broken down before the detergent reached the nation's water and, don't forget, the fishes' water. As little as one part per million of the detergents of the fifties reduced oxygenation of water by almost half, so that natural purification was set back seriously. The moral of this story is that industrial chemistry could have thought ahead much better than it did. The profits were enormous both in anticipation and realization, and the research toward producing nonpollutant detergents could have been undertaken before the damage was done.

Water as a scarce commodity was never considered to be much of a problem in Britain, but the expanding demands of industry make us realize how careful we must be with it. Haphazard, unthinking pollution of rivers is something we shall soon be unable to allow. Upland water must be conserved and not used for industrial process that merely needs raw water rather than pure water. Happily, our growing dilemma is calling forth more coordination between water authorities and water-using interests. Water conservation will redound to the benefit not only of wildlife conservation, but to visual amenity and recreation. Our need will cause us to spend the money, some of which would have gone a lot farther in an earlier day.

One more aspect of water use in our technological world is causing us to think hard, namely as a cooling agent. The warmed water runs away in rivers and into the sea and is changing the ecosystems of these habitats. Further, have you ever thought of low-temperature heat as a prodigious item of waste in our economy? We do not seem able to recycle it.

Advanced technology would have been unlikely to escalate had there not been a large population to absorb it and the world population would not be what it is had not technology made it possible. Are we confronted, therefore, with the revolting picture of the two serpents ingesting each other from the tail end? The nearer they come to what is presumed to be desired success, the more congested the picture becomes. What is going to happen? We do not know. The serpents must either unwind voluntarily, choke explosively, or wither gradually. I believe we are in this condition of the serpents, with very little time in which to take the first course. Choking seems to me more probable than withering. Choking is not a simple bit of physiology, for several systems of the body are involved. It is possible that the snakes could survive, but for a long time they would be very sick serpents. They might even learn not to do it again but to live in a non-self-consuming harmony.

Pollution is one of the major factors of development that could bring us to either the explosive choking or the slow withering. The car with its imperfect internal combustion engine is the cause of a large part of present-day pollution. The most visual aspect of this is in the smog which lies like a blanket over so many cities in which the world population congregates. Los Angeles, California, appears to be the ultimate in idiocy of city development. It lies in a broad hollow and the city is now fifty miles across, laid out on the grid pattern, most of it very much alike. It is an area of frightening monotony which some of us are even more frightened to think we see in sections of the inhabitants. Los Angeles is the paradise of the automobile and such are the climatic and topographical conditions that the gaseous automobile wastes, the dust in the air and the sunlight combine to form smog.

It has been said sardonically that people in Los Angeles like to see their air, just as smoke over the Black Country a hundred years ago meant activity and prosperity of a kind. Carbon monoxide, carbon dioxide and lead spread over our cities and either side of busy highways. California, having been one of the loveliest places in the world, drew in an immense, non-integrated population of people which sprawled over the state in a devastating way. My colleague, Raymond Dasmann, was moved to write a book which he called *The Destruction of California*. It is always worthwhile to observe examples of the ultimate: it is the ecological slant of mind to find them.

California in its state of stress and distress has produced some good forward-thinking minds who have much to tell us on community development, communications and pollution. It is in California that the start will be made with scrubbing the exhaust gases from automobile exhausts to make them less toxic and less destructive of the environment. London has done much by smoke abatement laws and zoning, but in the annual inspection of all British cars over three years old, the exhaust system of the engine is entirely ignored. Diesel trucks can apparently eject dense black fumes with impunity and badly maintained private cars inadequately consumed fuel. Once more, California is thinking ahead to a phasing out of the internal combustion engine in cars, and we should not forget that two large automobile manufacturing firms in America are going to modify their engines to use leadless fuel. Here is industry acting voluntarily to curtail pollution.

Escalating technology has produced many of the enveloping forms of pollution we deplore, but, as I have just said, it could be turned the other way as well, if we are willing to pay for it. When we say, "We've never had it so good," could we not see also that we have never had it so bad? So little of the so-called goods would need to be sacrificed to relieve some of the threats of envelopment by pollution. If it is true that pollution costs Britain about 250 million pounds a year, and I have no reason to doubt it, surely it ought to be possible to offset this in considered cost-benefit scenarios.

Two forms of world pollution that have received wide publicity are those of radioactive fallout and the diffusion and persistence of pesticides. There is a dramatic quality about this kind of pollution which makes a supine inhaler of smog into an ardent crusader for a cleaner world. Much of the literature has had emotional overtones. The scientist regrets incitement to emotion and would prefer that reasoned statement should be sufficient to cause a change of mind. Unfortunately, the possibly less scientifically equipped publicist must usually precede the scientist in arousing attention. Rachel Carson was an exquisite writer and held a degree in biology: her book *Silent Spring* did more to move official attitudes in the United States than more erudite scientific opinion.

I remember being asked in a committee in Britain what I thought of the book. My answer was deplorably equivocal, for I said that although I would not have liked to write the book myself, I was very glad it had been written. And so I remain glad.

Much fuller and more factual accounts of the pesticide story are to be found in Robert Rudd's *Pesticides and the Living Landscape* and Kenneth Mellanby's *Pesticides and Pollution*. Britain is showing exemplary action over curtailing use of the organochlorine pesticides. Many are now outlawed and have been withdrawn by the manufacturers. Public opinion has cut down the use of many others. Gardeners are of two kinds I always feel: those whose garden is an oasis and sanctuary, a pleasance you might say; and the other kind who stalks around his garden, spray gun in hand, as if it were a besieged fortress.

An ecologically balanced garden, one of checks and balances, will keep you busy, but you will get something of all you garden for, including a diversity of birdsong. To keep your garden free of dangerous insecticides is a positive act toward wildlife conservation. It is a sobering thought to remember that seals in the

Arctic and penguins in the Antarctic have DDT in the fat of their bodies. This stable substance has certainly got around the globe.

Commercial development of the organochlorine pesticides which have caused all the trouble has been a story of testing "candidate" substances for immediate toxicity in the laboratory, followed by field tests of a few days to a month. The results were not more than short-term toxicity studies; chronic toxicity studies would have taken two years. The ultimate refined assessment was consumer use. In other words, the public was the final guinea pig. Britain was saved what the United States suffered, by her diversified and rotation-conscious agriculture, and by the prompt action of the Nature Conservancy. The future, I think, will see these persistent substances being phased out. Once more, better early research and forward thinking could have saved much trouble.

Radiation is the other pollutant which rouses emotion very quickly. Damage by radiation is cumulative and when it has occurred is, so far, irreparable. To all intents and purposes, our fears are concerned with radioactive fallout, the dust that eventually comes to Earth after nuclear explosions. The so-called atomic powers have realized the danger to a considerable extent and have voluntarily restricted such explosions. They have also shown more foresight than has been usual in disposing of atomic wastes, but such disposal is still a major problem. Old coal mines would be so useful but for the fact that reservoirs of underground water, which we are going to need increasingly, would become contaminated. The abysses of the oceans have been dumping grounds, but Britain now constructs stainless steel containers for the waste, and these are improving all the time. It has been said that when the casings do eventually disintegrate the degree of radiation will have much decreased and that the remaining radioactivity will be small. The British atomic authority questions this and goes to immense trouble to store wastes adequately. Processes have been and are being developed to convert these wastes to chemically inert glassy solids to be stored in specially constructed tunnels.

However, one fallout component, strontium 90, has serious biological implications. Having affinities with calcium, it can enter the grass that cows eat and the milk the cows give, and the bones which the milk-fed children grow. Barry Commoner of Saint Louis, Missouri, who has become one of the leading world spokesmen on pollution of all kinds, made a collection of children's milk teeth, millions of them, and was able to show the general presence of strontium 90. He demonstrated the consistent under-estimation of the soil content of strontium 90 by the U.S. Atomic Energy Commission. His work so roused the mothers of the United States that as a result all testing has been much better controlled of recent years. The state of Alaska was particularly concerned because of an ecological finding that lichen absorbed particularly large amounts of radioactive fallout. Lichen is a major food of caribou and reindeer, and Eskimos and Lapps feed heavily on these animals. Thus, the bones of people in the Arctic who eat animals which eat lichen will contain a higher content of strontium 90 than those of people farther south.

Pollution, you see, has entered the wildernesses of the world, and is a function of the technological exponential which is in danger of enveloping us. I must say more than I would wish on pollution because so much of it is invisible, and some deplorable effects are delayed or apparent only when ecological equilibria have been upset. If such upsets are irreversible, impoverishment of our planet has taken place. As a world problem, pollution and population pressure are partners, spectral and sinister. The question is whether they are going to shrink our lives to a condition of life in death, or do we look outward and proclaim that we live in a beautiful world in which we believe and which we intend to maintain?

IV

GLOBAL CHANGES:
ACTUAL AND POSSIBLE

THERE ARE PROCESSES going on in the world that are not obvious to many of us, but they are of great importance and sooner or later we shall have to decide which way we are going. I have spoken of the enveloping character of advanced technology and the choking side effects of pollution. There is another aspect of this especially affecting large bodies of fresh water such as the Great Lakes of North America, at least one of the Swiss lakes, even the new Lake Kariba in Africa and perhaps surprisingly our own Loch Leven in Scotland.

Lake Erie is now looked upon as the classic

world example of the phenomenon of eutrophication—a sort of pathological overfeeding. Sewers and industrial wastes went into the lake for years, which meant an excess of some plant nutrients, some animal poisons, and an upset in the natural oxygenation of the water. Fish life has gone, there has been a dense blooming of algae—microscopic waterweeds—in the summer and, of course, people do not swim in this great lake anymore. There has been a further dumping of phosphates into the lake since detergents were used, and a vast quantity of nitrates coming from the use of nitrogenous fertilizers on agricultural land. Lake Erie is one of those ultimates I have mentioned before, which we should concentrate on as examples of what can happen to places.

In Europe there is Lake Geneva, a very pleasant place, and when I stay on its shores I much enjoy the delicious lake perch which the French and Swiss cook so well. But the human settlements around the lake are growing bigger and denser; there the oxygenation of the lower levels of the lake is failing, through increasing depositions of pollutants. The lake perch, living in an increasingly shallow layer of water near the surface of the lake, are growing less numerous. Shall I one day attend a board meeting of the International Union for the Conservation of

Nature at Morges on the northern shore of the lake and find I can no longer have a dish of lake perch? My gastronomic disappointment would be as nothing to my sorrow that a rich lake was now dead. It probably will not happen in my time but the process is well on the way.

Lake Baikal in Siberia is a very wonderful place with its own species of seal and unique ecological conditions around its shores. Industrialization has begun and there are the first signs of eutrophication. The Russians are not blind to this and are monitoring the situation carefully. We shall see what the possession of absolute governmental power can do in preventing the disaster that has already befallen Lake Erie.

Then there is Lake Kariba in Africa—a new multipurpose artificial lake. As it filled slowly, the catches of fish were most promising. Indeed, some species of *Tilapia* were introduced to take advantage of the quantities of fish food that could be expected. But the catches are not being maintained. Here eutrophication of the Lake Erie type is not taking place but an excess of plant growth is appearing and there will certainly be some ecological problems to solve in maintaining the multipurpose of the lake.

Last of these examples of what can happen to fresh waters is the relatively small Loch Leven, which lies between the Firths of Forth and Tay, in Scotland, with its world reputation for trout fishing. The fish have always been reckoned of good size and there have been plenty of them. The lake is set in a fairly rich farming area, which means the land has been well farmed in the past on traditional lines of plenty of stock and plenty of farmyard manure on the land. That kind of farming meant that the soil had a good humus content and acted as a sponge, letting run-off water gently into the lake. The land is still well farmed, but now the farmers are using a vastly increased quantity of mineral fertilizers, which means a greater run-off of water containing nitrates and phosphates. In 1948 I wondered about this change in the environmental conditions of the loch and hoped it was going to mean just more nutrients for the plankton and ultimately bigger fish. But the process ran ahead too far: there was the initial phase for which one hoped and then a fall. There came the algal bloom and a dense growth of bottom plants with less light for the insect populations, the larval stages of which were important fish food. This fishery is of such importance that special care is now being taken about effluents, but the story shows how tender and sensitive are fresh waters to the treatment they get from humanity.

I should also mention that in Lake Michigan the Coho salmon was introduced years ago to fill an ecological niche that, strangely enough, had not been filled by nature. A valuable new fishery was created, but that has now gone. There is so much DDT in the water and in the food of this predatory salmon that the fish itself is now considered dangerous as human food.

Now, there is a much greater change to which we are contributing, this time in the planetary atmosphere. You might call it pollution in a way, and in another way it is a dilution or a concentration. And our paradoxical friend and enemy the internal combustion engine is contributing all the time. I am alluding to the rise in the level of carbon dioxide in the atmosphere, a rise coincident with that of the consumption of fossil fuels—coal and oil. Of course, if there were double the amount of carbon dioxide in the air than there is, it would not interfere with our health in any way as far as we know. But in the biosphere as a whole carbon dioxide is powerful stuff. There is a carbon dioxide cycle which naturally keeps levels right. It is a system of great age and stability which we are now taxing with the immense amounts of carbon dioxide we are adding from the fuel we burn. Vegetation is a great buffer: the forested wilderness removes a great deal of the carbon dioxide by the photosynthetic activity of the leaves, turns it into wood, and so sequesters it, giving out oxygen in exchange. It happens that a higher carbon dioxide content of the air creates a greenhouse effect, favoring tree growth, which locks up the carbon again until a lower level is restored. But unfortunately we are cutting the virgin wildernesses all the time and reducing tree cover in so many places.

The oceans also soak up carbon dioxide and lock up carbon in the deeps. But the increasing concentration of carbon dioxide in the air leads to a gradual warming of the oceans so that they can hold less. The activities of industrial and technological man in our day are adding carbon dioxide and also injuring the capacity of the biosphere to redress the balance. All combustion is burning carbon or its compounds in oxygen— a single jet plane crossing the Atlantic uses thirty-five tons of it—and we are reducing the kind of plant cover which would help lock up the carbon dioxide produced. Suppose some bright scientist discovers some method of artificial photosynthesis which does not involve the return of oxygen to the air; he might be heralded as a genius because this would provide food quickly for the starving hundreds of millions, but it would effectively prevent the possibility of a posterity for them through the depletion of our atmosphere.

We are not yet at the end of this story. The warming oceans would alter considerably the distribution of the marine fauna. This has happened already in this century in the warming of the North Atlantic Ocean and has interfered with existing fisheries. Of course, through time fisheries adapt to new conditions, but there is another adaptation that would be much harder. The warming oceans and atmosphere would mean a recession of the polar ice caps. The Greenland ice is 9000 feet thick, so if that were to melt, with an equivalent melting of the Antarctic ice, the level of the oceans would rise considerably. Our ports would go under quite literally, and with them vast tracts of fertile soil. What happens then to the swarming human population? I suppose they move upwards and back, very slowly, of course, but surely. And what then?

Some scientists are thinking about these phenomena, but not nearly enough data are being gathered, nor monitoring being done. How far, really, do we think for posterity? The carbon dioxide problem is as yet remote. So often I have heard it said, posterity must look after itself. I can think of no more callous viewpoint. The sins of our forefathers now descended unto the third and fourth generations were largely the consequence of the sins of ignorance. We are ignorant no longer. Science enlarges our vision, and ecology is concerned with causes and consequences on a broad front. We should be delving ecologically into the future, but in general we are not doing so.

There is a subject nearer at hand but concerned with a shorter-term future, the field of international development. Agriculturists, engineers, marketeers and so on use their technical skills to devise schemes that will provide food, power, employment and industrialization for what are called underdeveloped countries. Perhaps it would be only a cynic who would say the real problem is of too many overdeveloped ones. Britain was early in this field and still pursues overseas development in a starry-eyed missionary spirit rather than a realistic one. I could list half a dozen fiascoes caused by blinkered thinking, and there are dozens more.

The Conservation Foundation, which I serve, recently helped to organize a study conference on the ecological aspects of international development. We were concerned with the integrity of the environment which should be a primary responsibility of an advanced nation. Some of us could feel little but shame at what man was doing to his planet. Ignorance now is culpable, but we are not ready to admit this. I have touched on worldwide pollution through the use of insecticides; there are other aspects of employing these substances, namely, that ecological balance is upset almost immediately, with the likelihood of repercussions, and there has been the most interesting scientific phenomenon of rapid genetic adaptation by insect pests to the insecticides being used. Indeed, the insects can almost beat the chemists who are developing new insecticides.

Cocoa was introduced as a new crop in Sabah, part of Malaysia, in 1956. By 1966, 6000 acres of virgin stands of splendid forest had been felled and planted to cocoa. Bark borers moved in as pioneer pests; getting rid of these by handpicking was too costly and by 1959 this was replaced by blanket sprays of DDT and Dieldrin. Several new leaf-eating pests began work that year, followed in 1961 by a plant hopper which sucked the shoot tips. Then several species of bagworms appeared and the silken bags of these caterpillars gave them an excellent protection against insecticides. Finally, when the situation seemed near hopeless, it was decided to stop spraying. Recovery was rapid because the natural predatory insects recolonized the area. The bagworms were controlled first by natural means and the other pests came down either to tolerable proportions or were controlled by selective, carefully timed insecticidal attack, devised by ad hoc research. Mass control on lines of blanket spraying is bad tactics. The strategy should be one of minimal use at critical moments.

Irrigation has been one of the great developments of this century although it is one of the oldest of man's achievements. Sumer and Egypt used their great rivers for seasonal inundation, but the modern methods involve continual irrigation and the use of concrete channels from stabilized watercourses. The disease of schistosomiasis has been endemic in Egypt, but its incidence has been moderate except in areas of perennial irrigation, such as the Delta. The disease is extremely debilitating and is caused by a tiny parasitic worm, the alternate host of which is a small water snail. Seasonal flooding does not favor the snail to the extent that perennial irrigation does. And as a result of irrigation the disease has now spread the length of Africa to an alarming extent, and in perennially irrigated areas the fiber of the people is being sapped. There is almost 100 percent infestation in the Delta where sanitary measures are almost impossible to implement because of the high water table and the seething population. In Upper Egypt the new Aswan High Dam devel-

opment will certainly increase the intensity of
infestation. Rhodesia is suffering appreciably.
Intensity of infestation in human beings is bring-
ing about hitherto unexpected complications in
bodily expressions of the disease.

And there is another problem. For each new
area that comes under irrigation, some land
from earlier schemes goes out of cultivation by
salinization and waterlogging, millions of acres
for example in West Pakistan. Furthermore, it
might be mentioned that the impoundment of
water in the Aswan High Dam is having a
serious effect on the eastern Mediterranean sar-
dine fishery. Once more a source of protein is
being given up for more starch. The Mekong
River in Southeast Asia and the curious inland
lake system have, through history, sustained a
quite amazing fertility of land which might be
expected to deteriorate under the conditions of
cultivation. But the overflow of the river in the
monsoon deposits new silt on it each year.
Further, the lakes are replenished and their
biological productivity is phenomenal, and undoubtedly made possible the Khmer civilization
of a thousand years ago. Now a series of dams
on the river is projected, which certainly will
provide power but will retard the flow of water
and may well reduce the fertility of the lands
formerly flooded naturally. Happily, a group of

ecologists has got in there this year, but whether in time to modify these great measures of change we do not know.

The underdeveloped nations, so-called, may be very rude to us of the West, but they have a perfervid belief in our technology. And were we to try to explain that we were not quite so sure of our cleverness, that we have made some deplorable mistakes, it would be interpreted as one more example of the West wanting to deny the benefits of technology to the rest of the world. We in the West are in a dilemma and some of us know it.

There is indeed a growing unsureness in the world. Recently the Conservation Foundation arranged an almost impromptu discussion between eleven people to examine the possible common fields between medicine, ecology, psychology, anthropology, architecture and landscape planning, and what is generally understood as conservation. We had a stimulating day and a half, but quite early in the proceedings members of several of the disciplines represented came around to a sense of impending tragedy which each of us felt. Basically, it was caused by the population problem: none of us could see that the world would escape the horrors of famine on a large scale. Indeed, there will probably be a succession of famines, but they will be no cure of the population problem. If 10 million were to starve to death in India this year, the population would still be greater at the end than it was at the beginning of the year. But it seemed to us that the very large catastrophe to which we were heading would not happen as a result of any one cause, but as a culmination of several factors, famine, war, pestilence, pollution and so on. A breakdown in technology, such as the New York-New England blackout of November 1965 could be the precipitating factor in a society geared to the electronic control of so much of the machinery of living. There could well be a chain reaction around our paradox of a globe, this close-knit, shrinking world which exhibits ever greater unfriendliness between its constituent peoples. This too is a fact of social implosion.

The ecologist sees the decline of the great natural buffer of wilderness as an element in our danger. Natural wilderness is a factor for world stability, not some remote place inimical to the human being. It is strange that it has been so long a place of fear to many men and so something to hate and destroy. Wilderness is not remote or indifferent but an active agent in maintaining a habitable world, though the co-operation is unconscious. Only we are conscious of what we are doing and capable of forecasting the consequences.

Pragmatic man, typified by too many of our politicians and those considered to have their feet firmly on the ground, has his head in some world of illusion of his own making. What is the use, he asks, of all that forest if it cannot be brought to the service of man? The answer is that it is already in the service of man if he is willing to accept fellowship with the world of nature. The forest is generous: it can spare him some trees for his timber, and all the time the silent forest is busy, giving us our oxygen, taking away the surplus carbon dioxide, helping to remove the pollutants. The hedgerow trees of England were never more valuable than today— nor the hedgerows—yet a misguided government department can give 50-percent grants for clearing what is called scrub. Even visually the trees are beautiful and stress-relieving, but in their silence they do much more. Their only voice is the wind; they have no vote and are defenseless. The practical man (who Disraeli said was he who could be depended upon to repeat the mistakes of his ancestors) can remove what is the nation's heritage and nature's tool to allow the easier passage of some mechanical Moloch.

Once more, the press of people. Mr. Robert S.

McNamara, who leads the World Bank, recently delivered a lecture at an American university. It was terse in quality, the most direct statement yet by any statesman of his kind. He is committed to development, but not development that is despoliation, and not development designed to catch up with population increase. He said quite plainly that the birthrate must be lowered, because the food per head of the world's population today is already less than it was thirty years ago. He points to the parsimony of governments of developed countries in devoting money to research in population-related phenomena. As he put it: "Hundreds of millions for death control. Scarcely 1 percent for fertility control." He adds that the threat of unmanageable population pressures is very much like the threat of nuclear war, and that the threat of violence is very much intertwined with the threat of undue population growth. Mr. McNamara added one hard truth, that "no reduction in birthrates has yet been achieved anywhere in the underdeveloped areas which can significantly affect overall world population totals."

He professes himself still to be an optimist and rightly argues against the belief that development must of necessity mean more population. He thinks it evident in the poverty-stricken countries that lack of development means continuance of the high birthrate and, I might add, of habitat destruction.

I suppose I am not an optimist, nor my friends at the Conservation Foundation whom I have mentioned. We are not alone in our pessimism. Lord Snow has also given a lecture to an American college and called it *The State of Siege*. He admits that he and some of his fellows have felt an uneasiness deepening, that we "are huddling together in our own little groups for comfort's sake." He feels the threat of population out of control and the thought of large-scale famine appalls his civilized mind. Where Mr. McNamare is optimistic is that the genetical breakthrough in producing new strains of wheat and rice will boost yields by half a ton per acre throughout Asia. Only 200 acres of these new strains were planted in 1965 but 34 million acres was the estimate for 1969, though much of the wheat- and rice-producing areas have not yet changed. Lord Snow has also heard about this breakthrough. It gives him a glimmer of hope if we in the West will help ourselves, and if the poor countries reduce or stop their population increase. Mr. McNamara must take the stand he does, because, as Lord Snow says as one more free than Mr. McNamara, we have to act as if the solution envisaged by both of them is more likely to occur than it is.

This always troubles me, the necessity of expressing faith which at bottom I do not feel. I am guilty of this private lying to myself over conservation of wildlife in Africa, and the latest news is that the Ngorongoro Highlands may be developed agriculturally. A watershed of high forest on friable volcanic soil which affects water relations far afield may be destroyed to grow more maize for a swarming population of a long line of destroyers, the forest-edge cultivators. Doubtless Mr. Julius Nyerere still believes in the Arusha Manifesto he signed with others in 1961, and which we of the West cheered so loudly as the dawn of a new era; his philosophical conviction will remain undoubted, but like the western politician I described earlier he must smile apologetically and say the present necessity demands this destruction of what should be our posterity's heritage. "Needs must when the devil drives," my grandfather used to reply to my idealism of childhood.

What I imagine to be the closely similar guarded optimism and reserved pessimism of Mr. McNamara and Lord Snow seems to me to take insufficient notice of the time factor, and because they are not ecologists they ignore the destruction of life-giving wilderness. The trouble is upon us and the several changes of custom and attitude are not going to take place soon enough. My friends and I of the conversation I described were all except one of the opinion that the real trouble would be upon us this century, probably as a social implosion triggered off by one of the factors to which I have alluded. Student unrest, black power and violence by spectators of sport are all implosive signs of over-large numbers.

As Mr. McNamara, Lord Snow and we were talking, a Soviet Academician, Andrei Sakharov, published a paper of strikingly similar sentiments. He is a pessimist but believes that extrication from our plight *is* possible if we move quickly enough, if the rich and poor nations of the world join in the endeavor. *If* we got to work and dropped the nonsense, Sakharov sees this as being possible by the end of the century.

But have we got as long as this to achieve the unity of action that McNamara, Snow, Sakharov and a few more of us see as the prime necessity? I cannot answer yes or no to this question. It is the continuing urge and the answer to why do we, who think this way, go on working as if the catastrophe would not come? We are human and a unique blend of optimism and pessimism which probably has evolutionary value. Also, we are fallible, but reason and intuition make us state the situation as we see it in hard terms. That group of us discussing the future knew we were among the fortunate, living in a still beautiful world. Is it love of beauty that moves us to the effort, because we know beauty is denied to so many of our fellow men?

V

THE FORWARD VISION
IN CONSERVATION

WILLIAM THE CONQUEROR made the New Forest his playground. He chose well, knowing nothing about wildlife conservation and such ecological notions as habitat, community and succession. Normans and their ancestors the Vikings were plunderers and destroyers rather than conservers. Nevertheless, the forests, chases and parks that the Normans reserved in England for their amusement have stood us in good stead a thousand years later. The New Forest is on poor gravel overlying an impervious clay, a horrible place agriculturally and I cannot believe William ejected many farmers, because the Saxons had a good deal of ecological sense. Let us be thankful it became a Royal Forest and has remained so till our day, being now the playground of a lot of people, a truly wonderful place for growing trees and a considerable haven for a representative sample of England's wildlife. It is a big enough place to have some ecological power of its own to retain its integrity.

The New Forest is not a British national park, a national nature reserve, or a Forestry Commission holding as a whole. It is the New Forest and a place of which we should be proud. Of course, in time of war busybodies without knowledge chirrup about the necessity of growing food and the apparently lazy New Forest had to give up some of its lawns. And they did grow their sugar beet and whatnot eventually. The Commoners had looked after themselves by stipulating that at the end of the war the land should be laid down to grass again and the fences removed. They also got an agreement with the Forestry Commission to keep the commons clear of tree growth in return for other areas devoted to trees. Well, after the war the commons were put down to good grass with the help of phosphate and potash dressings. Ponies, cattle and sheep liked this, so much so that they concentrated on the commons that had been plowed and reseeded, not doing the grass much good, nor themselves finally, because such concentration soon meant heavy infestations of parasitic worms. Meanwhile those poorer commons, left unplowed and almost deserted by the opportunist stock, began to grow a good stand of regenerating pine trees, a situation the forester likes to see, but this conflicted with the commission's agreement to keep these commons in grass. This foolish story of imagined patriotic expedience is a good example of the results of lack of any prior ecological study of land use and a long-range plan. The Verderers of the New Forest had learned their empirical ecology the hard way, and their good sense was too easily interpreted as reaction and inability to understand the national urgency.

That was over twenty years ago and the New Forest has in some measure settled down again. What must now be the principal worry of the Verderers is the vastly increased visitation by people from elsewhere, many seeking that which the New Forest gives so generously, some of them imagining that when you get out of your car you make whoopee, and some quiet, decent but ignorant folk can soon create a lot of damage. The Verderers, and foresters of the Forestry Commission, are patient men: they manage, advise and clear up. They do a good job of educating the public and cooperate with the Nature

Conservancy, which in Great Britain is the governmental body charged with tasks of nature conservation and research.

That is my impression of one splendid piece of England, but all in all England is losing out in her countryside. The Town and Country Planning Act of 1947, at first an excellent brake, has worn thin but still does good. When it comes to export or die, another facet of the population problem, economic growth overrides everything. We are still adding to that quarter of a million acres of dereliction. Housing and factory development need land. New and widened roads plow through the countryside. It has been firmly instilled into us that we cannot stand in the way of progress, so-called. You cannot anyway, because we live in our era, but a large body of private and professional people in this country do influence the decisions of governments and developers and help to save a little more of the heritage of England for a longer time. Or so we hope, despite the awful future of the world I have been dolefully retailing in these chapters. This is the human spirit that could make surer our posterity.

It is so easy to descend into a series of ineffectual flapping movements: I have already said I intend to continue motoring at over forty miles and hour, and because I live deep in the country our sole household help is electricity. So I am interested in better roads and new power stations and make my contribution to pollution in the countryside. Those with whom I associate do not wish to put back the clock, nor do we wish to enjoy the benefits of technology so long as the factories and power stations are fifty miles to leeward of where we live. That again would be the siege mentality. The art of conservation stems from the science of ecology, a delight in knowing how nature works and a love of beauty which may or may not be conscious. Every acre, not only of Britain but of the globe, demands thought before its biological and visual relations are altered.

Conservation in the sense it is generally used now arose in the United States in Theodore Roosevelt's presidency. A large part of the United States had taken an awful bashing from the exploiters; wildlife was getting scarce and timber was being used almost for the sake of using it, to keep the forest felling going. It is one of the unfortunate paradoxes that a conscious sense of conservation seems to come only after a long period of devastation has made the need apparent. We ought to be able to do better than that. It is thirty years since Jacks and Whyte wrote their classic book, *The Rape of the Earth*, in which they gave it as their opinion that of all countries South Africa had suffered the worst devastation at the hand of man. Well, today South Africa is one of the most conservation-conscious countries in the world.

Britain, though she began the Industrial Revolution and devastated landscapes in the northern counties, enjoyed such a good climate that some scars were soon healed and a great deal of the country remained beautiful, for the Anglo-Saxon seemed to have an innate ecological sense of fitting his villages and buildings into the right place in the landscape. So it took us another thirty years after America to think seriously about the subject. We nearly left it too late, but now that we are in it, I think we are doing well, though not well enough.

I remember Herbert Morrison entertaining us in Downing Street when the Nature Conservancy was founded. He was very kind and told us that he thought nature was very important. I had no doubt of his conviction, only of his understanding of what it was all about. I respected him deeply for his open mind, which helped so much to establish the Nature Conservancy. He loved his walks in the Green Belt of London.

Almost immediately the conservancy took its stand as a research body in a subject that needed both study and good will to make it

effective. The National Nature Reserves that the
conservancy set about acquiring varied in size
from a few acres to many thousands, and there
were some public misgivings when it was found
that these areas were not national parks. They
were chosen as habitats, in which research for
the better care of the country at large could be
carried out. Much of this research has been what
is sometimes called pure research, but some of
it from the beginning was mission oriented. Of
course, what appears pure today is applied
tomorrow.

For twenty years the conservancy has pro-
gressively realized that conservation is not just
the importance of nature and all that, but a
concern with the human being and his habitat,
a concern for the survival of the human species
on the planet from the environmental viewpoint.
Sometimes nature has to be protected *from* the
human species, and in conservation we do not
subscribe to any notion that nature is worthy
of protection merely *for* the enjoyment or education of the human being. Nature exists in its own
right and our attitude to it is a measure of our
consciousness of the whole situation of which
our own survival is a part, not be-all and end-all.

It is natural that each nation should have its
own approach to conservation. England established a National Trust as long ago as 1895. Its

first objectives were to care for the history and beauty of the country and encourage public appreciation. The movement has been enormously successful in the presentation of English country houses in their setting. This was environmental conservation with a special slant.

The National Trust for Scotland first followed a similar course but in 1943 appointed a committee on wildlife conservation, and I would say that the Scottish Trust now leads the world in the wholeness of its approach to environmental management. There are the individual Scottish houses and their gardens and treasures, but it also looks after whole villages and small towns. The Scottish National Trust has also shown a readiness to join with other bodies, interested for example in ornithology, in running the bird sanctuary and inhabited island of Fair Isle. The remote and spectacular island group of Saint Kilda is managed in partnership with the Nature Conservancy. Very soon a large district of the West Highlands will be run as a joint effort in multiple land-use management, the three owners being the Nature Conservancy, the Forestry Commission and the National Trust for Scotland. They may be joined later by some private owners.

Just after World War I the Forestry Commission started as an organization designed to grow sticks of timber. But since those pioneer days there has been a drastic change of outlook. The commission is in the forefront of dedication to the philosophy of multiple use. It preceded state action in establishing its own National Forest Parks, which in Scotland have to make do for the national parks that country has been denied. Further, in the last twenty years the commission has planted its new forests with much more ecological awareness, using different species from acre to acre as the soil dictated. This has resulted in a considerable increase in the beauty of our countryside because, let me emphasize, much of what we call beauty in the countryside stems from conditions of ecological repose. We sense the beauty even if we have not a clue about the ecology.

In England the National Parks Commission was a political sop to a popular idea. The English national parks were really regional parks, and the commission had little money or executive power. Care of the parks and provisions of recreational facilities have been quite inadequate. The men have been devoted but governmental backing was timid and parsimonious. This situation has changed in that the National Parks Commission has now been replaced by the Countryside Commissions. With the change, we are hoping for a much more vigorous interest by the British government in environmental affairs. There is, governmentally and publicly, an increasing awareness that what was called "nature and all that" is a natural resource that has to do with national well-being.

"The Countryside in 1970," as it is called, is a conference that has been in constant session for several years, and which held formal sessions in 1964 and 1967, and will presumably meet again for a grand winding-up in 1970. Under the chairmanship of H.R.H. The Duke of Edinburgh it has been an excellent device for coordination and publicity. Through these years, Prince Philip has allowed no hot air, only good crisp statement and argument. The cooperation of the national industrial boards in the conference has been a distinctive feature. What happens after 1970 remains to be seen, but in some new form the conference will need to continue, because 1970 marks no millennium. The fact that the Council for Europe has made 1970 European Conservation Year is also significant.

The urge is there all right, and a lot of first-class scientific data, but not enough people, either in or out of power; nor do those in development industries have a sufficient sense of urgency to value and preserve our remaining bits of wilderness for their beauty, their air-

and water-purifying action or their value as study areas.

The International Biological Program, which has been in operation for some years, has as its title, "Biological Productivity and Human Welfare." An understanding of the energy flow of ecosystems is an essential part of this worldwide cooperation, and the Terrestrial Conservation section is stimulating international effort toward acquiring sites that may be said to exhibit natural ecosystems at work. It has been emphasized that I.B.P.'s activities in this section must cover the whole Earth. Experience in this international venture reveals how rapidly natural ecosystems are being destroyed. I feel that the next five or ten years will be crucial.

Turning now to other countries: the United States has been in conservation as a direct effort since 1910 anyway, but at that time there was very little scientific research on which to base conservation as an applied science. There was great activity in wildlife research, but the more fundamental work on the dynamics of ecosystems as applied to conservation seemed to lag. The leeway is being made up now and the National Science Foundation, with its large government funds, is doing a splendid job of evaluating proposed researches and supporting on an international scale those that come through the careful screenings.

National parks constitute a particular United States contribution to world culture. The 3200 square miles of Yellowstone in Wyoming were established way back in 1872 and the process is continuing, with many millions of acres involved. In addition there are many sizable wild-life refuges for particular species or groups. These have no absolute sanctity, but once established they take quite a lot of undoing.

The biggest headache for the U.S. National Park Service is how to handle visitors. In the early days it was necessary to persuade people to visit the parks; now with a total of around 150 million visitors, the necessity of canalizing traffic and building hardtop paths in fragile habitats is urgent. In this branch of management the National Park Service today is creating an expertise of which Britain is only slowly becoming aware.

Since the inception of the International Biological Program there has been a strong movement in the United States to get representative ecosystems set aside as such on the same lines as the Nature Conservancy has followed in Britain. We all know how difficult it is for a government agency to make a quick decision, and part equally quickly with a sizable sum of money. Because of this we lose potential valuable sites. In the United States there is a very useful independent body also called the Nature Conservancy. It is in effect a rolling fund guided by people with good ecological knowledge. When some place of unique value is threatened, the American conservancy can jump in, buy an option pending survey or can buy the lot. The property in question is then handed over to the state agency most concerned and the purchase price is repaid in the time it takes for the money to be forthcoming. The National Park Service has been handicapped in the past by inability to act quickly on buying inholdings in national parks. The recent establishment of the National Parks Foundation with a good rolling fund will do for the parks what the Nature Conservancy does for other properties of ecological value. A similar type of fund is much needed in Britain despite the existence of the Town and Country Planning Act.

Russia tells us very little about what she is doing, but we do know that she is committed to conservation from an entirely hardheaded point of view. The Russians see quite plainly that many natural resources which we might consider only from the aesthetic point of view can be made to yield a crop to mankind and still not lose aesthetic value. By their action with the

Saiga antelope of the steppes they have conserved a diminishing stock till it now reaches three million head and yields half a million carcasses a year for food and skins. This can be a surer way of conservation than relying on sentiment. Sentiment and ethics should never be confused. Ethics stand firm and are to be sought by spiritual and intellectual effort of reflection; sentiment is a poor guide in the mosaic of ecology and conservation.

Ecologically, as well as politically, the eyes of the whole world are on Africa. What are the new nations going to do with their continent and its incomparable wildlife resources? My own feelings are mixed as to the role played in the past by the colonial powers during their administration. Most British administrators wished to do the right thing by both people and wildlife, but if they had to choose one or the other they usually rather pompously choose people. The administrative group, always the decision-makers, were not scientists and the principal technical services were agricultural and veterinary. The agricultural officers were not scientists either, and saw the continent in terms of bags of maize, bolls of cotton, and cattle, sheep and goats. The veterinarians saw the tsetse fly as a prime enemy and the wildlife as carriers of disease. It was not until the 1950s that ecologists from Britain and the United States really had a chance to show the wide spectrum of hoofed animals in Africa as an interlocking guardian complex of the habitat, making a much better job of biological productivity than the intruding cattle, sheep and goats. Looking back now, it is surprising how quickly the scientific attitude caught on in Africa. It is the accepted way now, but the wildlife is in as great danger as ever, or more so, because the population is increasing so fast.

As the countries of Africa gained independence, there was a voluble call from the western world to save the wildlife. Many well-known figures wrote eloquently to the effect that the wildlife of Africa was a world possession, a resource in which we were all concerned. Mr. Kenyatta picked this up immediately and in a very clever statement to the Arusha Conference of 1961 put the ball back in the white nations' court by pointing out that if African wildlife was indeed a world possession, it must be a world responsibility to pay for it. The West gulped once or twice but on the whole the richer nations have stumped up rather well.

National parks in Africa are an interesting story in themselves. The Belgians established huge and splendid ones in the east of the Congo. They exercised more power than the British were inclined to do, in that the Belgians decreed that the human being had no place in a national park. If they *were* there, they should be removed, and so they were. Human beings were not trusted vis-à-vis nature. I think this was mistaken policy, but the Belgian parks were undoubtedly magnificent, even into the time of independence. In South Africa the Kruger National Park is best known, but it is only the largest of many in that country. The magnificent Ngorongoro Crater was excised from the Serengeti National Park of what is now Tanzania even under British rule, but the Serengeti Plains still provide the greatest surviving pageant of the migrating herds in Africa.

Naturally, we are all glad about the national park movement in Africa, but for myself I do see dangers. I have heard men who ought to know better say the future of African wildlife lies in the national parks. This puts the animals into enclaves, or at worst, ghettos. If representative African wildlife is to survive, there will need to be many more national parks than there are now, and that is scarcely likely. Alternatively, the value of wildlife as part of the biological productivity of a region and its place in protecting such habitat as cannot be successfully brought under intensive agriculture must be realized. Immense areas of African soil are poor and lateritic and if they are bared to agriculture or wrongly grazed, they become bricklike and their last state is very much less productive than their first.

I once read in what was intended to be an authoritative report that as there were so many hoofed animals in Africa obviously there must be great scope for stockbreeding. This is a quite fallacious argument, and fortunately the report had no great influence. The ecologist has a moderately good hold in Africa these days and there is a strong pro-wildlife interest abroad in the world, but I repeat, world opinion should not sit back feeling that its job is done with the establishment of national parks. We in the West pay for African wildlife and rightly, but the ultimate criterion for survival is the human population. If that rises for another thirty years as it is doing now, all the efforts of the past fifteen years will be to no avail.

The International Union for the Conservation of Nature is only twenty-one years old. It runs on a shoestring but as a clearing house and a finger on the pulse of world affairs in wildlife conservation it has done a remarkable job. Gone are the days when *protection* was in its title instead of *conservation:* the world has awakened to the main ecological fact, that protection of any one creature or a complex of species depends primarily on persistence and survival of the habitat. That is conservation and it applies the world around, from Tropic to Arctic, from the deep ocean to the seashore.

To sum up: I am not utterly pessimistic, but there is not the slightest justification for any smug, starry-eyed satisfaction that the world's wildlife is now safe in our enlightened care. Time is not on our side and our present enlightenment may not go far enough.

VI

WHERE DOES
RESPONSIBILITY LIE?

THE EUPHORIA of landing on the moon has been less hallucinatory than that of the flight of the first man in space. Ten years of this extraordinary way of getting around have almost got rid of the notion that if we wear out, eat up and generally defile our very unusual planet we shall be able to blast off to some other virgin globe. The Earth is our home; it was made ready for the rapid evolution of exploiting man by many millions of years of organic activity. Man had no place in an earlier world.

There may be other planets we can live on, reached in travel time longer than our normal life span, but the chances of our reaching a new world precisely at a time when man could make good use of it are remote. If advanced or even primitive cultures were present, should we employ forthwith the weapon of war to make room for ourselves, or should we exercise our usual unctuous hypocrisy of washing our hands in imaginary soap and water?

We can set aside this kind of daydreaming and make up our minds that our concern is here on Earth insofar as persistence, nutrition and social well-being are our aims. Some economists and organic chemists have forecast the possibilities of extreme densities of human beings on our Earth which is over two-thirds covered by ocean, and assume that a social adjustment in our mentality will evolve as rapidly as our numbers increase. This seems to me unlikely and as an ecologist living on a known Earth now well surveyed from the air, and even minutely by satellites, I am bound to continue thinking in terms of solar energy and photosynthesis by chlorophyll. And I see these not only in terms of possible food production, but in the power of the forest wildernesses to be storage banks and regulators of our vital atmosphere, and our rising to continual awareness of the nobility of wilderness. Mere food plants would not act as such a store, because our bodies would recirculate the products so quickly. Energy flow and recycling is of the essence of organic existence, but there are different rates of flow.

In plain terms, we cannot give up our world to the production of human beings; yet, as I have said, the biggest problems facing the world today are the continuing rise in human population, the continuing rise and diversity of pollution, and finally, the increasing difficulty of preserving examples of the world's natural ecosystems with their species of plants and animals. Insofar as the world of man is prepared to concede this last to be a problem at all, its gestures are patronizing and conciliatory rather than actions of prudence in conserving as wilderness those portions of our planet which the ecologists of all men are now making articulate. "Speak to the earth and it shall teach thee" is the task and reward of the ecologist, but as he learns these truths of the wilderness silently contributing to man's own existence, his knowledge also becomes his sorrow and burden as he sees the wilderness recede.

Increasing population for years ahead is an inevitability; pollution need not increase, and were we ready to accept the idea that technology should use its own inventiveness resolutely to clean up after itself, we could have a healthier and more beautiful world within a reasonable time. There is an ethic of responsibility for the environment which is a growing body of philosophy, but it is not generally understood and it is followed only expediently. Did I not admit to using gas containing lead, and that I fly 50,000 miles a year? Yet I am supposed to be in the spearhead of thought and action attempting to contain the pollution, and wondering how we can contain the population. I repeat that I live in my era; I could do no good by following the ultimate misapplication of logic by walking out naked to live by my beliefs, for I should be naked also of many of the skills of the savage in collecting his food and trying to live from a depleted wilderness. Nevertheless, it still does behoove me to continue in the field of discovery and probe intellectually into an emergent ethic.

I believe that thought on the problem of population has been too pragmatic, though understandably so. Any intellectual change of attitude might take a long time to filter through society, but such change must carry a conviction from within and a priori, quite distinct from hope of benefits to be derived.

For many years I have been interested in the patterns of sexual convention in human beings and the phenomenon of reproduction. Though sexual intercourse is still necessary for reproduction, reproduction is not necessarily the desired end of love-making. Religion has often wished to imply that whether desired or not, reproduction should be accepted as a consequence not to be hindered. Even among the many who do not feel that way, and with the great advances in the techniques of contraception, there is insufficient acceptance of the idea that sexuality is something existing in its own right, not to be confused with and clouded by unwanted reproduction. The necessity in our present world problem is to accept sexuality in this way, untrammeled by doubt. The extreme right wing of religion would imply that man should be able to rise above the animal function of sexuality except in the service of reproduction. The extreme left of behaviorism on the other hand would say, of course sexuality is animal and so are we, and therefore we should be free to exercise it as animals.

The animal quality is the common factor in these two views, but I think they are both mistaken. Why not look upon human sexuality as something that is potentially uniquely human? Presumably, the feathers of a bird first developed as a form of insulation against heat and cold. Feathers as a means of flight were an entirely different development, but they still continued to serve the function of insulation. A third entirely different function has developed in the patterns and colorings of feathers which have become means of recognition and of conveying signals as in display and in the almost unison of action in a flying flock. The other functions remain, nevertheless. There is nothing teleological about this, of course, just natural selection upon existing natural equipment. I think human sexuality should be looked upon in this way, that as an adjunct to reproduction was its first function, it is not necessarily its final one.

The phenomenon of human love has been observed for a long time in our history, certainly ever since we had means of conveying our thoughts through the instruments of speech and then writing. The great love stories of the world have a warm place in our hearts, even in periods and cultures where love by equal choice has been uncommon. We do not doubt the existence of love. At its highest, human love is exclusive and absolute, as expressed by Lancelot in his love for Guinevere. He could not go through the act of love with any other woman, even when such an act would have liberated him from captivity to continue his mission to rescue Guinevere, who was about to be burned. And you will remember the story of the paternity of Galahad, when Elaine had no power over

Lancelot until magic was employed to deceive him into thinking Elaine was Guinevere.

Nowadays we profess to believe in falling in love as the basis of marriage. Love as part of the expression of sexuality is the added human function which the act holds above and beyond the reproductive function which should be exercised so rarely. Within the ideal, by which I mean the relationship of love between two people which leads to that exclusive state, sexuality should not be restrained but let free for its influence on spiritual development between the sexes. Modern contraceptive technique and the emancipation of woman in our age make possible this emancipation for man and woman together, of reproduction set in its right perspective. I consider the fears sometimes expressed of the dangers of such freedom becoming available to the adolescent as being quite prurient. Leave them alone, with the example of parents in love.

If our culture learned the potential quality of human sexuality as part of its very being, it would be more helpful in the world at large where population control is even more urgent than it is here. It is time that church and behaviorism dropped the "animal" connotation and thought more of the uniquely human potential of developed sexuality not bound up with reproduction. The sexual act between lovers is of the very essence of unselfishness. The rare intention to conceive would then be approached as a sacrament of joy, rather than the possibility of conception being feared as the cloud of so many lives.

I have heard it said that the constant sexual desire of humanity is one of the crosses we bear. I would rather consider it the other way around as one of our greatest potential gifts. Over thirty years ago the anthropologist J. D. Unwin wrote of the drive of peoples in which there was apparent greater restriction of sexual freedom. The Epicurean and the Stoic would agree with that, and so would I, if restriction comes from within and is not imposed from without, because the spiritual force of human sexuality is within love and compassion and the naturally exclusive ideal. Within these restrictions there can be no overindulgence because the individual appetite takes care of that. The human being ennobled by the sexual selflessness of love is ready to be the servant of his world. Promiscuity is dissipation of creative force.

An ethic of sexuality joined with an ethic of the wholeness of life, giving us a reverence for lowlier forms, and reacting on population growth or limitation, should influence the attitudes of the West toward our exploitation of land and animal life. We are degrading animals in our day by the methods of reproduction and rearing we are now employing. Debeaked hens, cooped-up calves fed on antibiotics and our growing denial of the personal association to our domesticated animals, which is their right if we domesticate them, constitute degradation not only of the animals but of ourselves. On these systems individual keepers of animals are not thinking in terms of starving millions but of profits easiest gotten; our acceptance from our positions of remoteness encourages these practices and so does governmental acquiescence, because governments really are fearful about what starving millions might do. When I read in a scientific journal of a bull in its brutish decency ultimately declining to serve the canvas cow and the rubber tube, and having to be chased around a paddock with a stick to make it do so, I say that civilization is failing. Artificial insemination of cattle can be a force for good, but bulls should not be brought to a state of revulsion, to give us our "pint-a-day" and all that. All governments should boldly face their responsibility to work out population and nutritional policies, not play the opposite game of subsidizing irresponsibly reproductive families.

Is vote-catching to the incurable weakness of democracy?

There is the third ethic of the land, our responsibility for the environment of the human species now and in the future. Such qualified pessimism as I have voiced in these chapters allows no relaxation in our care for the face of the planet in a problematic future. Care of the wilderness is part of that environmental conservation in which we now include the human being. The exclusion of man from the hierarchy of nature, so common in the past and even in our own time, is to put him in the position of a bourgeois rentier, living off an economy but having no responsibility for it. To make him an integrated functional member of the planet and animal world about us is no denigration of his high estate, no assumption of a mealy-mouthed egalitarian folksiness. Rather does man accept his position in nature as the species granted the privilege of fulfilling the aristocratic ideal of noblesse oblige, of being the servant of his people.

This is our responsibility toward the Earth and its denizens. We shall doubtless make honest mistakes in our exercise of service, but that it where research itself is no luxury, only one part of the fulfillment of our obligation. I have expressed my doubts whether we shall have a

long posterity if we continue as we are doing,
living off the capital of the world's ecosystems
that evolved long before we were consciously
men, throwing our poisonous refuse into air and
water arrogantly as well as in ignorance. In the
fulfillment of our humanity we should act as if
posterity stretched into infinitude, and by thus
acting we shall make this more possible. We
know that the evolution of our species probably
rests now in the psychological and, as I believe,
in the spiritual sphere, and we have so far to go.
When the apocryphal Midwest farmer, contributing by his practices to the eventual Dust
Bowl, said, "Posterity never did nothin' fer me,"
he was indeed turning his back on the evolutionary potential of his species, selling his birth-
right for a mess of pottage. We have seen in
recent years a deep questioning of the attitude
that natural riches are there for the exploitation
of man. A less anthropocentric philosophy of
restraint, of identification with, rather than exclusion from, nature is developing its own ethic
of love.

If we accept the philosophy of respect for
life with its view that organisms exist in their
own right as fellow members with us in the
world community of living things, we must be
guided constantly by the discipline of ecological
observation, otherwise we are in danger of

being rather silly. Man as an omnivore becoming philosophically a hypervegetarian does not reach his own ideals when he swallows lowly and invisible organisms on his lettuce, and the Jain bent double peering at the ground before each step lest he should kill anything would need eyes of an order not granted to us to see the still smaller creatures in his way. There is no room in our philosophy of responsibility for preciousness. We tread and eat and live as man, prepared to kill if the necessity or inevitability is there, but not for fun.

The American ecologist Aldo Leopold was in my opinion the clearest exponent of an emergent ethic of the land. He said, "That land is a community is the basic concept of ecology, but that land is to be loved and respected is an extension of ethics . . . We abuse land because we regard it as a commodity belonging to us. When we see land as a community to which we belong, we may begin to use it with love and respect."

The form and style of the land is part of our environment as surely as the community of living things. Landscape is near and touching to some of us, a constant and urgent concern as of someone we love. To others it does not seem to have this quality. You remember the Yorkshireman's comment on seeing the Lake District in an earlier day: "There's nowt'ere but scenery."

Yet even if not of conscious concern to enough people, landscape is of importance. The reciprocation of conscious concern is of the very nature of love, which is essential to all human relationship.

Perpetuation of a derelict landscape as a background to children's lives is like rearing them to some extent in lovelessness, even if a rusting motorcar body does provide a lot of fun. Sometimes when I see examples of presumed art made up from the scrap-iron dump and hear music not unlike the sound of a tin can being kicked down some sunless alley, I feel that perhaps this is what must happen to the sensitive child reared in the industrial miasma. They have to express themselves and this is how they express the upwelling of art, having no sense of season, flower or flow; there are only staccato skylines and cacophony and an outraged Earth.

By definition, landscape architecture carries the connotation of artifact. If man enters into landscape at all he in influencing and reshaping it. If he merely exploits a landscape he is almost certainly degrading it and making it less beautiful. If he lives with it as a husbandman calling it home, he will almost unconsciously produce many of the rural landscapes and small towns of Europe which we find pleasing and which we know to be biologically productive. Sometimes landscapes have been engineered, but rarely of more than a few hundred acres in extent. Most of these we find pleasant, but they were made for the favored few. We have now reached a point in time when we can deduce the history of land, and insofar as the land use has been deleterious we have sufficient ecological knowledge to architect the landscape on a regional plan for biological productivity and the content of man. Human tastes vary, but all in all the most general consensus of beautiful landscape would be found to be that which is in ecological repose or near to it.

Ian McHarg, a Scotsman who found freedom to work and develop his thought in America, has become an outstanding voice in this field, a highly individual one trying always to justify his ecological planning of landscape by return to basic principles of interrelationships and interdependencies within the site. The placement of buildings and their design, in following ecological principles, can so often be justified aesthetically. Whether we are conscious of it or not as subsequent observers, most of us find this kind of landscape architecture to be satisfying. The odd and the idiosyncratic rarely give content, and the bull-at-a-gatepost method of carving a landscape usually ends up in real trouble. McHarg's new book, *Design with*

Nature, is at once a testament of belief backed by well-chosen case histories, and a thing of beauty in itself.

I have said little of the wilderness as a place where such men as can should spend their forty days alone or with a companion. This is a time for re-creation of the spirit for which too few men find opportunity. Whether it is forest, mountain or desert is immaterial as long as the wilderness is not a man-degraded one of recent time. I do not wish to dwell on this aspect because the fulfillment of it is the privilege of the few and I have an uneasy feeling deep down that we should not burden the wilderness with this egocentric human purpose. The wilderness does not exist *for* our re-creation or delectation. This is something we gain from its great function of being, with the oceans, part of the guardianship of the world in which we have come so recently to be a denizen.

The true natural wilderness from which we have carved our precarious plenty cannot be re-created in our time, possibly never. But that which we have taken from the wilderness we can treat with gratitude and responsibility. The full awareness of what man has done in creating dereliction and squalor has only come in our time. There has also come the knowledge of how to cope with it. The great earth-moving

Barr, J. *Derelict Britain.* London: Penguin Books, 1969.

Carson, R. *Silent Spring.* London: Penguin Books, 1965.

Commoner, B. Science and Survival. London: Ballantine Books, 1971.

Conservation Foundation, The (Sir F. Fraser Darling, Chairman). "Implications of Rising Carbon Dioxide Content of the Atmosphere." New York: Conservation Foundation, 1963.

Cook, R.C. *Human Fertility: The Modern Dilemma.* New York: Sloane, 1951.

Darwin, C. *The Origin of Species.* London: Collier-Macmillan, 1962.

Dasmann, R.F. *The Destruction of California.* London: Collier-Macmillan, 1967.

Elton, C.S. *Animal Ecology.* London: Chapman & Hall, 1966.

——. *The Ecology of Invasions by Animals and Plants.* London: Methuen Educational, 1958.

Errington, P.L. *Muskrat Populations.* Ames, Iowa: Iowa State University Press, 1963.

Inge, W.R. *Outspoken Essays.* 1st and 2nd series. London: Hodder & Stoughton, 1919 and 1922.

Jacks, G.V., and Whyte, R.O. *The Rape of the Earth.* London: Faber, 1939.

Leopold, A. *Sand County Almanac.* London: Ballantine Books, 1971.

McHarg, I.L. *Design with Nature.* New York: Natural History Press, 1969.

McNamara, R.S. "An Address to Notre Dame University." 1969.

Malthus, T.R. *An Essay on the Principles of Population.* 5th ed. London: Murray, 1817.

Mellanby, K. *Pesticides and Pollution.* London: Fontana, 1969.

Population Reference Bureau. Population Bulletin 25: 1-21. Washington, D.C., 1969.

Rudd, R.L. *Pesticides and the Living Landscape.* London: Faber, 1965.

Snow, Lord. *The State of Siege.* New York: Charles Scribner's Sons, 1969.

Vogt, W. *Road to Survival.* London: Victor Gollancs, 1949.

——. *People.* London: Victor Gollancz, 1961.

MORE BALLANTINE
CONSERVATION TITLES

THE ENVIRONMENTAL HANDBOOK, edited
  by John Barr   40p

The 1970's is our last chance for a future that
makes ecological sense. The book focuses on
some of the major problems of our deteriorating
environment, and — more important — suggests
action that can be taken immediately in any community, by any individual. Foreword by Kenneth
Allsop, and contributors include Sir Frank Fraser
Darling, Dr. Paul Ehrlich, Lord Ritchie-Calder,
Professor René Dubos and Dr. Kenneth Mellanby.

THE POPULATION BOMB, Dr. Paul R. Ehr-
  lich   30p

Overpopulation is now the dominant problem in
all our personal, national, and international planning. Dr. Ehrlich clearly describes the dimensions
of the crisis in all its aspects, and provides a
realistic evaluation of the remaining options.

THE BEARS AND I, Robert Franklin Leslie 40p

This book has been hailed as the North American "Born Free", and is the story of how one man in the Canadian North woods prepared three orphaned cubs for the perils of living free. His account of how he raised the three bears takes place over three years — a continuing adventure that involved forest fire and perilous canoe trips — and, above all, an unforgettable experience in the potential relationship between man and his fellow animals.

NEVER CRY WOLF, Farley Mowat 30p

Never Cry Wolf is a charming and engrossing scientific study that explodes the myths many centuries old about wolves. Far from being treacherous and vicious creatures, the author reveals that the wolf family he studied could be a model for its human counterpart in its loyalty, responsibility, hospitality, child-rearing practices, and even sense of humour. It is the true story of one man's incredible adventure with a family of wolves in the Arctic wilderness.

FURTHER CONSERVATION TITLES
FROM BALLANTINE BOOKS

Friends of the Earth

The present environmental crisis is only now being recognised as an ultimate threat to man's survival. We are finally becoming aware that the land, sea and air on which we depend cannot tolerate the sort of abuse we have subjected them to.

Action is required now to develop a way of life based on sound ecological principles and related to the limited capacity of the earth to support the human species. To place our faith in growth in the Gross National Product as a measure of our welfare and happiness, and in technological solutions to all our problems, is proving disastrous to the environment.

It is one thing though to lament the tragedy of dying rivers and the curse of industrial dereliction, but quite another to choose an issue, fight the case, and win. Any campaign for a better environment must make sure this is an issue which decides the fate of politicians, activates complacent authorities or closes factories.

This situation needs new organisations uncompromising in their defence of the environment and uninhibited in the action they are prepared to take.

Friends of the Earth Ltd. is one of them. It is an international non-profit making organisation prepared to take aggressive legal and political action to ensure a better environment for everyone. In the UK it is formed as a company limited by guarantee so as to fight freely and quickly.

We are not just idealists, but we do have ideals. We place emphasis on practical action and we recognise the need for many new organisations to share the work. We are also aware of the need to give more help to existing conservation groups, which have been labouring long and hard. Our Earth is threatened and needs every friend it has.

FOE intends firstly to pursue an active publishing programme with Ballantine Books, to provide the best possible information, written for the intelligent layman, about the remedial action required to meet current threats to the environment. We intend to encourage further research aimed at a greater understanding of the impact on the Earth of Man, and his technological society. We shall also urge action now, based on what is already known, to resist the use of a given technology without proof that it will not cause lasting harm.

Unhampered by any party-political allegiance, FOE will undertake substantial legislative activity, including lobbying and focusing public attention on critical issues. We will join other organisations in going to court to fight environmental abuse. We shall wage an all-out war on any interest which ignores the needs of the environment.

FOE's members will form specific task forces supported by teams of environmental experts and citizen's groups. The acronym FOE is appropriate: any friend of the earth must be the foe of whatever or whoever degrades the earth.

FOE needs support. It has a growing register of Friends who are prepared to fight authorities and industries insensitive to the ecological effect of their activities. If these goals are yours, contact us by completing the form and sending it to Friends of the Earth, 8 King Street, London W.C. 2. Tel. 01-836 0718.

FRIENDS OF THE EARTH

8, King Street,
London WC2E 8HS

Registration as a Friend ....
Friend and Supporter £3 ....
Friend and Supporter £100 ....

Name: ....

Address: ....

....

Tel. No: (day) .... (evening) ....

Interests and/or specialised knowledge or training:

Ideas for action:

All cheques should be made payable to Friends of
the Earth Ltd. As a company limited by guarantee,
all money FOE receives must be devoted to its
objects and cannot be distributed.